UNDERSTANDING THE RIOTS

LOS ANGELES BEFORE AND AFTER THE RODNEY KING CASE

BY THE STAFF OF THE LOS ANGELES TIMES

Los Angeles Times
A Times Mirror Company
Los Angeles, California

Los Angeles Times

Publisher: David Laventhol
Editor: Shelby Coffey, III
Senior Editor: Noel Greenwood
Assistant Managing Editor for Graphics: Terry Schwadron

Project Director: Angela Rinaldi, Los Angeles Times Syndicate
Text Editors: Tim Reiterman, Karen Denise Robinson, Jim Schachter
Graphics/Production Editor: Michael C. Chaplin
Photography Director: Larry Armstrong
Photo Editors: Mike Edwards, Con Keyes
Writers: Edward J. Boyer, Janny Scott, Mark A. Stein, Robert W. Welkos
Copy Editor: Jim Hollander

Design/Production/Printing: Graphics Management, Inc.:
Production Supervision: Bill Dorich
Art Director: Patricia Moritz
Color Separations: Tru-Colour
Printing: Northwest Web

ISBN # 0-9619095-9-5

Copyright ©1992, Los Angeles Times.

Published in July, 1992 by Los Angeles Times
Times Mirror Square, Los Angeles, California 90053

A Times Mirror Company

Cover Photo: J. Albert Diaz
Inside Cover Photo: Ken Lubas

Printed in the U.S.A.

4   From the Editor

6   Prologue

9   1   "BURN, BABY, BURN"

22   2   A CHANGING MOSAIC

33   3   THE PATH TO FURY

45   4   "MY GOD, THIS IS IT."

67   5   AWAKENING TO A NIGHTMARE

98   6   "...CAN WE GET ALONG?"

120   7   BROOMS, BUCKETS, COOLING EMBERS

142   Epilogue

144   Perspectives

MAR. 3

From the Editor

Those first days and nights of the riots that shook Los Angeles in the spring of 1992 were a mixture of tension, horror and surrealism. Our deepest concerns at the Los Angeles Times were for our staffers who went out into the streets gathering news and sometimes coming directly into the line of fire.

Photographer Kirk McKoy had a pistol emptied at him at nearly point-blank range.

Reporter George Ramos wrote about having a gun aimed at his chest.

Photographer Gary Friedman turned around at one intersection after taking a couple of pictures to find a shotgun aimed at him.

Reporter Jim Herron Zamora was slugged and wrote a harrowing piece about being in the middle of a fracas. Someone on his left shouted, "Get out of the way. Let me get a clear shot." The bullet just missed Zamora.

Photographer Rosemary Kaul came under fire returning from the demonstration at police headquarters.

Messenger Gary Dunn and Sandy Kay from the Art Department put out a fire in a first-floor office at Times Mirror Square.

And reporter John Mitchell—with courage and grace—risked the wrath of an angry crowd to rescue a Vietnamese refugee.

And these were not the only Los Angeles Times people who came under fire or risked heavy stones, shotguns or pummeling. People who produced and distributed the paper each night faced many of the same dangers.

As a paper, the Los Angeles Times received the full measure of its staff's heroism—and its professionalism. What the paper didn't want were any more bronze plaques honoring journalists killed pursuing news—plaques like those in the lobby of The Times, which itself was burst into that first night.

What was needed was what the staff of The Times gave in great measure:

The freshest news.

The clearest analysis.

The focus on the people.

The voices of America's unresolved urban, social and racial issues.

The heart of the dilemma and the heart of the city.

People from all parts of the Editorial Department—from Ventura to San Diego—volunteered and poured in.

The compliments they received have been resounding. People like Dan Rather of CBS, who called after the first night to say he had never seen a paper mobilize for that big—and that complicated—a story that fast and that well. Harrison Salisbury, one of the legendary American foreign correspondents, told one of our critics that the L.A. Times' reporting on the riots was some of the best he had ever seen.

But beyond those big names, what is most memorable are the calls of gratitude and concern from readers—the quiet people who call to thank you for explaining the complex and the overwhelming.

No doubt we did not do a perfect job. But, at the end of the day, what do you have in journalism except to bear witness, give voice, show truth, search for causes and re-examine effects?

The honor is to work full out, at the height of your powers, with good people beside you. The staff of The Times has done that. Years from now, those of us who were here for these days will remember the paper's pride amid the tragedy.

And that pride will stay engraved in our hearts.

This book is published in tribute to all who worked, and in gratitude that all came back safely—as on wings of eagles—to Times Mirror Square, where the Times eagle was and is still.

SHELBY COFFEY III
Editor and Executive Vice President

At the intersection of Florence and Normandie, one of the early flash points of the unrest, the anger of a crowd shocked by the King verdicts was unleashed with violent fury. Motorists were pulled from their vehicles. Protesters hurled rocks and bottles at passing cars, looted a nearby liquor store and torched some buildings. After the angry crowds left the area, there was little for police to do beyond directing traffic and standing guard at what was left of the nearby businesses.

Photo: Kirk McKoy

Prologue

"Not guilty. Not guilty. Not guilty. Not guilty…"

In a hushed Simi Valley courtroom the phrase rang out ten times that warm spring afternoon, Wednesday, April 29, 1992.

Those simple words—the jury's verdicts in the trial of four Los Angeles police officers charged with beating Rodney Glen King—unleashed a torrent of fury in a city that liked to show the world a face of multicultural tolerance.

The jurors' decision and the events it provoked shook Los Angeles as fiercely as the Sylmar earthquake in 1971, shamed it as surely as the night in 1968 when Robert F. Kennedy was gunned down in the Ambassador Hotel.

Unanimously, the jurors had voted to acquit Stacey C. Koon, Theodore J. Briseno and Timothy E. Wind of all charges stemming from King's videotaped arrest on March 3, 1991. Laurence M. Powell was acquitted on all but one count of assault. On that one count, the jurors told Judge Stanley Weisberg, they were hopelessly deadlocked.

Exuberant, Briseno leaped to his feet and hugged his lawyer. Powell embraced his attorney, too. Brimming with relief, the four officers slapped each other on the back while Powell's sisters and mother wept softly. The prosecutors, staring silently at the counsel table, hung their heads. The judge declared a mistrial on the single remaining count against Powell, thanked the jurors and sent them home.

Outside the courthouse, a crowd of at least 300—families from South Los Angeles, 43 miles to the southeast; Simi Valley homemakers; teen-agers circling on bicycles; veteran court-watchers—erupted in loud, angry debate.

As the officers and their lawyers left, the crowd surged toward them. Koon emerged from the courthouse, surrounded by sheriff's deputies and camera crews. "Guilty!" some people screamed, scuffling with the deputies as Koon and his lawyer darted for a car. Powell fled amid a hail of rocks. A few lone voices called nervously for peace and unity. But public sentiment was overwhelmingly against the verdicts. Forty-three-year-old Rose Brown of Los Angeles said America had been on trial. "I am not given to riot, but just you watch," said Brown. "Something's going to break."

Within hours, her premonition was fulfilled. As dusk fell, Los Angeles would evoke memories of another hot Wednesday, in August, 1965, when Watts erupted with an earlier generation's rage.

Outside the East Ventura County courthouse, reaction to the King verdicts was overwhelmingly negative. Pamela Jones of Simi Valley, right, and others who had gathered there expressed shock, grief and anger after the officers were cleared of nearly all charges in the videotaped beating.

About 500 National Guardsmen took up positions in the Watts area to help Los Angeles authorities restore order during the 1965 uprising. The riots—at that point the worst civil disturbance of the century—rocked the city and the nation and left 34 dead.

Photo: John Malmin

"BURN, BABY, BURN"

1

Urgent shouts, police sirens and the breaking of glass lured Nettie Lewis out of her modest apartment. Stepping into the too-warm summer night, she saw a bright orange fire billowing from the nearby White Front store. Hooper Avenue and 76th Street were filled with people, angry and energized with frightening power. A few sprinted from the blazing store, loaded with merchandise.

Lewis barely noticed. The 30-year-old woman—who had left a small Arkansas farm town called Hope 10 years earlier to come to Los Angeles—couldn't take her eyes off the searing flames that shot out of every door and window of the White Front's sooted silhouette. Unmoving, she stared absently, confused and disbelieving, until one of the looters nearly ran her down in his haste.

It was just past 8 p.m., Aug. 11, 1965.

South-Central Los Angeles was on fire.

An hour earlier, a routine traffic stop three miles southwest of Lewis' apartment sparked a wildfire of urban insurrection larger and deadlier than anything the United States had seen in this century.

At 116th Street and Avalon Boulevard, Highway Patrolman Lee Minikus had arrested Marquette Frye, 21, on suspicion of drunk driving. A crowd formed. Tempers flared. Frye's mother, Rena, and brother, Ronald, were arrested. Angry words led to spitting; scuffles escalated to rocks and bottles. After a tense few minutes, the CHP was able to withdraw with the suspects. But the officers left behind a critical mass of rebellion.

For six days, the black residents of Watts and surrounding areas burned, looted and battled with police, unleashing—in one fierce and frightening explosion—decades of pent-up frustration and anger. Raging men and women chanted a bitter chorus—"Burn, baby, burn!"—as they tried to pay back Los Angeles for a lifetime of abuse, of neglect, "of the dual justice in the system, of the lack of respect for everybody, of not following through on programs and promises that could have brought about something better," Onamia Bryant explained 27 years later.

Bryant—a Los Angeles schoolteacher now who worked as a shipping clerk and took night classes at Compton College when Watts exploded—viewed the '65 riot from the porch of her family's new house in the Athens District, looking on as looters pillaged a nearby shopping center. The city and the world watched these events in horror—and in fear. Thousands of National Guardsmen poured into Los Angeles to quell the disturbance. Bleary-eyed police, working around the clock, labored desperately to restore order. But Bryant and Lewis, like many other residents, sensed the anger was directed outward. They felt oddly safe.

"We weren't in the middle of it, so it wasn't so frightening to us," Bryant recalled.

The toll on Watts and the rest of South Los Angeles was heavy, nonetheless. By the time the riots had run their course, 34 people lay dead; 1,032 were injured and 3,952 arrested. About 200 buildings had been destroyed; 400 others were damaged by fire or looted. In today's dollars, the damage totaled a staggering $183 million.

After the embers cooled and the guardsmen and reporters left, the residents of Watts sifted somberly through the rubble. Gone was the 55th Street Drug Store, a musicians' haunt. Gone were such landmarks as the Avedon Ballroom, Little Harlem, the 54th Street Ballroom and the Safeway on Imperial Highway. Gone were the corner markets, the clothing stores, the shoe repair shops, the furniture marts. What had been 103rd Street was now known as "Charcoal Alley."

At the same time, leaders of the white Establishment scrambled to make sense of what seemed to them senseless, self-destructive behavior. Then-Gov. Edmund G. (Pat) Brown named millionaire industrialist and former CIA director John McCone to head a panel to study the riots. The McCone Commission's conclusions, published a speedy 100 days later, didn't surprise anyone who had spent time on Central Avenue. But it alarmed the rest of the city. Even behind its closed doors, and with only minimal community contact, the commission saw that the riot wasn't a product of wanton thuggery. It was "a symptom of sickness in the center of our [city]," the predictable result of the idleness and despair rampant in densely populated ghettos where "the conditions of life itself are often marginal."

Twice as many were jobless in South Los Angeles as in the rest of the city. Crowded schools produced dropouts. Discrimination corralled blacks in old and decrepit homes. Bus service was inadequate, stifling efforts to find jobs outside the area and fueling an incendiary sense of isolation from the rest of the city.

Black citizens had been saying the same things to anyone who would listen. The single-family houses and two-story apartment buildings of South Los Angeles were, no one could deny, a long way from tar-paper shacks and tenements. But they were just as far from the ranch-style houses for which California was becoming famous. The plumbing in about a third of South-Central homes was dilapidated—or altogether missing, according to a Census Bureau study. Local public schools were so underfunded and overcrowded that many were on half-day sessions, while white schools had empty desks. When it came to keeping blacks in their place, blacks would say, Southern California was not as brutal as the South. But the best jobs, the nicest houses, the finest shops were all off-limits to people of color.

The idea that Los Angeles was just another big city with fundamental urban problems was not easy to square with the city's image. Here was a metropolis practically invented by developers and movie stars—people not accustomed to unpleasant reality.

Early in the century, railroads enticed Midwesterners to the coast by making Southern California seem like an agricultural paradise, Valhalla with orange groves. Hollywood in the 1930s made Los Angeles glamorous and sophisticated. The economic boom experienced during World War II was echoed by

MAY 27, 1943

War contractors are forbidden to discriminate on the basis of race, speeding the migration of blacks to Los Angeles.

10

"No Negroes or Orientals Desired."

—Sign at entrance to Highland Park, 1958

a housing explosion that, when packaged in television programs, made L.A. the capital of the American Dream in the 1950s. A young city, it was a natural center of the youth culture of the 1960s.

One constant, maybe the only one, was size. L.A. was always big. And looking to get bigger. Of the nation's 15 largest cities, 14 lost population during the 1950s. Only Los Angeles grew.

That suited Timothy Howell just fine. Howell, an ambitious 18-year-old in 1958, hitched a ride to Los Angeles with his brother, a Navy man stationed in San Diego. When he pulled into town, he felt as if he'd landed in heaven. All those impossibly pretty pictures of L.A. he had seen in Detroit were real. This was someplace he could settle down, make a life and start a family.

It was like that all over South Los Angeles in the 1950s. Alone or with families, farmhands and factory workers were feeding a mighty river of migrants that doubled the black population of Los Angeles, to 461,000 people, in a single decade. The flow started in the '40s, when the number of blacks in L.A. had tripled, and continued into the '60s, when the black population nearly doubled again. For every black resident of Los Angeles County at the start of World War II, nearly nine blacks lived here 25 years later.

People of every racial and ethnic group were pouring into Southern California back then, of course. Veterans by the thousands were moving to the pleasant, bustling city of tomorrow they had glimpsed on their way to fight the Japanese in the Pacific. Here was a city where everyone, it seemed, could own a house, and every house had a garage, and every garage a car. Brand new, wide-open freeways were being built to whisk folks wherever they wanted to go. Smog was approaching lethal levels—1955 boasted the highest level of ozone ever recorded—but that could be interpreted as a sign of progress, too, couldn't it?

Thomas Souza certainly didn't mind the haze. His father, William, drove his family to L.A. from Boston in a 1953 Chevy fresh off the showroom floor. Thomas loved his new home. Everything was so new in the San Fernando Valley. In Boston, buildings were 200 years old. You didn't have a yard for your pet. You traveled in subway trains or buses, not Chevy sedans. California was different. Wide open. Big. Free. Everyone was from somewhere else. To 13-year-old Thomas, olive-skinned and scrawny, anything seemed possible.

The Souzas bought a 3-year-old, two-bedroom, one-bath house in Van Nuys, near where Vanowen Street meets Balboa Boulevard. But the spread set William Souza back a whopping $10,300. Helen, his wife, was not sure they could make the payments, so everyone worked. William Souza was a court clerk by day and a dry cleaner at night. The three boys delivered newspapers.

Thomas still found time to ride his motorbike on streets near his home. That was where he met his first Los Angeles cop. Souza doesn't remember the ticket as well as the man who wrote it. He looked so professional, the teen-ager thought, so ominous. Spotless clothes crisply pressed. Neatly knotted necktie. Shoes and belt so shiny you could see yourself. The uniform was beautiful. Just like on "Dragnet."

JUNE, 1943

Police round up gang members and weapons after sailors from the Chavez Ravine Naval Base attacked Mexican-American teen-agers. The incident launches the racial conflict that becomes known as the "Pachuco" or "Zoot Suit Riots," for the teen-agers' preferred attire.

JANUARY 11, 1944

The Joint Committee for Interracial Progress (now the county Commission on Human Relations) is established by the Los Angeles County Board of Supervisors, only the second such panel in the United States.

11

Police Chief William H. Parker, left,
shows Councilman Tom Bradley a
Molotov cocktail he said was pulled
from the ashes of a burned-out
building after the Watts riots. Parker
was testifying before a City Council
committee about the events leading
to the unrest.

Photo: John Malmin

In black Los Angeles, the LAPD forged by Chief William H. Parker had a different image. Just living in a predominantly black neighborhood seemed to invite police abuse; venturing out often guaranteed it. The McCone Commission report dismissed tales of widespread police brutality, warning that such charges could "reduce and perhaps destroy the effectiveness of law enforcement." But the "thin blue line" argument—which, like many of the notions in the McCone report, would resurface a generation later—was hard for many blacks to reconcile with their own experience.

Police routinely stopped and searched blacks who entered white neighborhoods. In black neighborhoods, treatment was sometimes worse. A month before the Watts riots, for example, a 21-year-old black woman said she had been raped by a white officer after a routine traffic stop early one morning. The accused officer failed a lie-detector test and resigned. The grand jury declined to indict him.

The LAPD also had a reputation, even among some of its black officers, for brutalizing black suspects. At the 77th Street Division in the years before Watts, it was common for white booking officers to harass black suspects. Insult them. Shout at them. The arresting officers would punch and prod from behind. Suspects either took it or they didn't. And if they didn't, if they made some kind of move, so much the better. Then the officers could really beat them. Sometimes they would shove the prisoner up to the booking window so the booking officer could slug him through the slot. Everybody at the station back then knew about it, but no one said anything. That, at least, is what black officers reported later, with regret. Black civilians in Los Angeles either lived it or believed it.

The residents of white Los Angeles, however, were blithely unaware of such conduct. It wasn't reported in the newspapers, and it wasn't part of their lives. Discrimination and poverty kept L.A. largely a segregated city. To whites, Los Angeles meant Disneyland and drive-ins or freshly turned earth that was an orange grove yesterday and would be a housing tract tomorrow. To outsiders, not yet infected with the cynicism of a later generation, the city's image—of a glamorous Oz populated by movie stars and beach boys—continued to be shaped by Hollywood myth makers.

Still, discrimination in Los Angeles was rarely as ham-fisted as it was in the Police Department; indeed, it was less of a problem here than most any other big city

Historian Carey McWilliams once attributed that relative broad-mindedness to the fact that Southern California—despite its Civil War sympathics for the Confederacy—was, by the middle of the 20th Century, dominated by integration-minded Midwesterners. Writers Arna Bontemps and Jack Conroy alternatively suggested that the apparent tolerance shown blacks may well have indicated simply that bigots had to spread their hatred among Latinos and Asians as well.

In an odd way, Timothy Howell was calmed by Los Angeles' peculiar strain of segregation. In Detroit, his middle-class family had moved into a white neighborhood in the 1950s; some of his 17 siblings were the first black students in a less-than-welcoming white high school. That was tough. Here in California, he had moved in with his sister in Compton, found work in a car wash and a laundry, then moved up to a civil-service job in the food service department of the Westwood Veterans Administration Hospital. Just like that.

Enough black people found a place in Southern California to maintain its gloss as a welcome destination for migrants from the South and Southwest—if only because where they came from was often so much worse.

Jake Flukers arrived in California a few months before the Watts riots and a year after graduating from high school in Eunice, La. He left for the West still smarting from a beating he and a friend had suffered at the hands of a white man who objected to them playing tennis with two whites at a segregated Eunice tennis court. Flukers, one of 11 children of a maid and a farmer, had deliberately integrated the public court to make a point with the small town's racists. A judge suspended his assailant's 28-day jail sentence, but Flukers learned something new about white people: When the first blows landed, a white woman unexpectedly raced to his defense.

"It made me realize all white people weren't racist," he said.

Flukers left Louisiana for California on a lark, to visit some friends from Eunice who had moved to Los Angeles and loved it. However, he found that even in Los Angeles, the best jobs had a way of finding white men to fill them; lesser jobs could pay as little as $1.25 an hour. Even at that, unemployment in South Los Angeles stubbornly hovered above 10%.

There was some hope for Flukers and others in the new federal anti-poverty programs that President Lyndon B. Johnson was creating. The assassination of President John F. Kennedy in 1963 was a major setback for blacks as well as a national tragedy; Kennedy had proven himself devoted to civil rights. But Johnson was going beyond civil rights, beyond voting rights: He was promising a War on Poverty, a Great Society. And this Great Society, he pledged, would finally include black people as equal partners. Jobs were the weapons in this war, and the new Job Corps was issuing arms.

Flukers enlisted.

In the Job Corps, the eager young man earned $30 a month, received free room and board and learned to weld. It wasn't much, but it was something. It taught him a trade and it taught him how to work. It gave him a good start—some self-discipline—and he appreciated it. "You see a lot of people my age who went through these programs who are living comfortably," he says today.

The problem was, the Job Corps and other programs were never as big as promised, certainly never as big as needed. In Los Angeles, federal programs by 1965 had created 363 low-paying, full-time jobs for young people and about 400 jobs for poor adults throughout the city. But there were 15,000 people without work in South-Central alone.

Money that might have been used to create more jobs was held hostage as

DECEMBER 24, 1951

Los Angeles police arrest and beat seven Mexican youths on "Bloody Christmas," leading to the indictment of eight officers and charges by Edward R. Roybal, the city's first Latino councilman, of systematic police brutality.

Amid the ruins of the Watts riots,
Tony's Shoe Shine Stand, in one of
the hardest-hit areas of South Los
Angeles, reopened for business. It
would take much longer, though, for
the area to recover.

U.P.I. Telephoto

With sporadic violence continuing, the National Guard gave many residents an added sense of security. On riot-scarred Wilmington Avenue at 103rd Street, a guardsman helped an elderly woman cross the street.

Photo: Bruce Cox

With the fires out and the violence abated, the business of rebuilding could begin. Pitching in first were crews from the Dept. of Public Works, who labored to clean up the area at 103rd Street and Maie Avenue in Watts.

Photo: John Malmin

Mayor Sam Yorty stubbornly resisted federal demands that poor and minority citizens have a say in how it was to be spent. Yorty had been elected in 1961 on a reform platform with minority support, but by the end of his first term four years later, the Congress of Racial Equality conducted a sit-in in his office to prod him to accelerate the anti-poverty programs. Meanwhile, Johnson and his War on Poverty were being derailed by the intractable, money-gobbling war in Vietnam.

As the programs faltered, they bred despair instead of hope. Rather than integrate society, they alienated further its most marginal segments. The poor and blacks—especially poor blacks—felt they had lost their best chance at working their way into the economic, political and social mainstream.

California voters fed those feelings. After Congress passed the Civil Rights Act in June, 1964, Californians turned around in November and overwhelmingly approved Proposition 14, a constitutional amendment that voided state fair housing laws. It was an outrageous insult, endorsed by The Times and made worse by the fact that the initiative so clearly violated the new federal civil rights law and was destined to be found unconstitutional.

But the proposition's legality was less important than the voters' mood—unsympathetic, even hostile. It was in evidence wherever the city's black residents looked, from the condition of their schools to their treatment by police to their opportunity for employment.

And as hard as it was on adults, it was worse for their children. Dispirited parents could not motivate dispirited students, many of whom recognized that a high-school diploma was not the same ticket to the middle class for them as it was for white students.

Test scores in Watts were as low as one-sixth of those in the city's best schools—schools that in the '50s and '60s were graduating many of the whites who would take their places atop the city's Establishment leadership in the '80s and '90s. In the inner city, many children simply gave up—on school, on family, on life. The McCone Commission ultimately would lament: "What has depressed and stunned us most is the dull, devastating spiral of failure that awaits the average disadvantaged child in the urban core."

And so Watts exploded in gunfire and flames, setting the national tone for a turbulent decade of defiance, militancy, impatience, disillusionment and re-evaluation.

JANUARY 28, 1963

Gilbert Lindsay is appointed to the Los Angeles City Council, the first black ever to serve as councilman. Tom Bradley wins election to the council three months later.

2 A CHANGING MOSAIC

On the heels of the Watts uprising came riots in Detroit, Newark and New Brunswick, N.J., Washington D.C., New York and other urban centers, redefining the civil rights movement. Following that long hot summer of 1967, President Johnson created a commission to look at the causes of urban unrest. The Kerner Commission concluded that America was in fact two nations: one black, one white, separate and unequal.

Meanwhile, angry students and activists flooded city streets and college campuses to demand an end to the Vietnam War and to protest social inequities. The Chicano movement swept across the West, demanding an end to unfair immigration policies, police brutality and discrimination. California's frightened mainstream responded with Ronald Reagan, the retired movie actor elected governor in 1966. He pledged to restore law and order, resist fair housing laws, make greater use of capital punishment and root out welfare cheaters.

These were years when the Los Angeles Police Department gloried in its tough image. By the time of the Watts riots, Thomas Souza was a Police Academy cadet. Officers, he remembered, were taught, "When you go, you go all the way. You don't go soft-handed. You don't try and show signs of weakness....Officer safety comes first. We don't care about criminals. You are worth 10 of them.

"We had the fastest response and the strongest officers," he recalled.... "When we hit the scene, people knew we meant business. There shouldn't be a piece of that suspect left." If you didn't jump into the pile with your fellow officers, he knew, you were considered less of a partner, one not to be trusted.

Tom Reddin, replacing the late William Parker as police chief in 1967, tried to change the storm-trooper look of his officers. In place of buckles on their Sam Browne gun belts, officers had Velcro-type fasteners; policemen derisively called them "Bruce Browne" belts. "He made us wear our name tags," Souza recalled. "I remember that was a big bone of contention. 'Why should criminals know our name?' " Police were told to get to know minority residents as something other than suspects. Many were put back on foot patrol. In a move applauded in poor black neighborhoods, patrol officers were directed to hand out warnings instead of citations for minor mechanical violations of the vehicle code. All this made for good public relations, Souza said, but in the minds of officers it did nothing to deter crime.

Three years after Watts, Souza was working as a motorcycle officer, with orders to ride his Harley-Davidson four times a night past the Black Panther headquarters near Central and Vernon avenues. "It was like wearing a bull's-eye," he said. There were "sandbags stacked up on the outside of the building up to about the windows. It looked like a machine-gun emplacement. There were no lights on inside. It had been in a few gun battles." That same year, 1968, three

Black Panther members were slain in a shootout with Los Angeles police.

The Panthers' premise was that the police—an arm of the oppressive white Establishment in black neighborhoods—must be monitored by blacks. And, if necessary, engaged. Their philosophy found a following in black Los Angeles.

One day, Souza and a partner stopped a black student to write a traffic ticket outside Jefferson High School, at 41st Street and Hooper Avenue. The youths who gathered around called them "pigs."

"I tried to handle it like a gentleman," Souza recalled. "I called the guy 'sir' this and 'sir' that. You know, like 'I stopped you for this, sir.' " As Souza handed him the ticket to sign, the youth walked over to his car, pulled out a napkin—maybe it was a rag—came back and used it to hold the officer's pen. He didn't want his skin to touch an object that an LAPD cop had touched. Then he threw the pen on the ground.

You didn't have to be a Panther to distrust the police. Southern blacks had grown up with police officers who enthusiastically enforced segregationist laws. And Timothy Howell, raised in Detroit, didn't trust the police either. He had returned to Los Angeles a week after the Watts riots, following a three-year stint in the Army. The LAPD frightened him, angered him, and several encounters with Los Angeles police in the post-Watts era hardened those feelings even more.

Howell settled his family on La Salle Avenue, in one of the many neighborhoods abandoned by whites in the wake of Watts. Howell, back working at the VA hospital as a pharmacist's assistant, and his wife, Joyce, a nurse, bought a seven-bedroom, two-story home. In the next 13 years, they would have 10 children. Education was drummed into the Howell kids. But even as Howell worked to ensure his children's future, he feared that a split-second encounter with police could undo all that he had tried so hard to accomplish. "I'm not going to see my sons shot down like dogs. Whatever the police throw at you—no matter how outrageous—do it," he told the boys.

Like thousands of Southern Californians—men and women of all races, but disproportionately blacks and Latinos—Jake Flukers was fighting in Vietnam rather than on the city's streets. Flukers saw his Army duty as a job. With combat pay, hardship pay and his regular salary, he made $700 a month. "That was a lot of money," Flukers said, enough money to send some back to his mother in Louisiana to help take care of his younger brothers and sisters. "It was an economic thing then just like it is now," he explained. "I had a friend who got killed going back to Vietnam for a second time just to get the combat pay."

When Flukers left for the jungles of Vietnam in 1966, he was a young black man filled with hope—proud of his country, optimistic about its future. But like so many of his comrades, he came back disappointed and disillusioned. "When I was in Vietnam, I felt that the struggle was over with," he remembered. "We were going to accomplish something as a people. I thought, 'No way will it ever go back to the way it was.' At the end of it, I started thinking the same things were going on."

FEBRUARY 27, 1966

The federal government announces a $7.6-million reconstruction project for Watts, where riot damage at the time was estimated at $40 million.

Part of Flukers's youthful enthusiasm died when a sniper killed civil rights leader the Rev. Martin Luther King Jr. in Memphis, Tenn., in April, 1968. The rest was snuffed out two months later, when an assassin killed Robert F. Kennedy in Los Angeles, minutes after the liberal New York senator had won the California presidential primary.

As the assassinations poisoned the dreams of a generation, the war in Vietnam undermined a society's best intentions. Southland defense factories were turning out jet fighters and missiles for the seemingly endless jungle war. But President Johnson's failing policy in Southeast Asia was dragging his entire Administration down with it, including the War on Poverty.

Still, blacks were getting a foothold in local politics like never before. n 1969, the same year men landed on the moon, a black Los Angeles city councilman named Tom Bradley—a former UCLA track star, ex-cop and lawyer—was drafted by the city's moneyed Westside leaders, at the urging of a South-Central minister, to run for mayor. Because he was smart, likable, steady and palatable to a white constituency, the Westsiders thought Bradley could be the balm to heal the city, to finally put Watts and race behind it. Mayor Yorty responded to the challenge by conjuring up frightening racial scenarios. He said that if Bradley were elected, white police officers would quit. Whites would not be safe from the black hordes. Bradley, he added, had ties to the Black Panthers and other radicals.

Bradley lost. But even in his defeat, black residents saw hope.

"When Bradley came close, I said, 'Any time a black man comes this close, he done won,' " recalled Art Washington, who had come to Los Angeles from Chicago following a fight with his wife two weeks after the Watts riots. "To me, the man had won, because we have to be twice as good as a white person to get a position like that."

Four years later, Bradley ran again—and won in a landslide. Los Angeles still was deeply divided on racial lines. But this time, polls showed, Yorty's racist rhetoric proved his undoing. Less than five years after Watts, Los Angeles—then the nation's third-largest city—had a black mayor.

High-rise towers soon sprouted on Bunker Hill. But South Los Angeles stayed in its slump. For three decades, the area's economy had been dominated by industrial plants owned by such corporate giants as General Motors, Firestone, Bethlehem Steel and Goodyear. Along with civil service, those factories—mostly unionized—let a growing black and Latino middle class accumulate savings, buy their own homes, educate their children and start businesses. In the '70s, however, the factories began to fold, usually to be replaced by smaller firms that paid less and laid workers off more suddenly. The same merciless economic disease that afflicted auto workers and steelworkers in the nation's Rust Belt spread unchecked through South Los Angeles.

Kerman Maddox's father felt the change. While Maddox studied in college, his father managed several small grocery stores. There were stark differences between his store in Long Beach, where aerospace and shipping companies were

AUGUST 29-30, 1970

An East Los Angeles parade to protest the Vietnam War turns into rioting that later spreads to Wilmington and South Los Angeles. Newsman Ruben Salazar, a leading spokesman for Chicano rights, is killed by a sheriff's deputy's errant tear-gas canister.

growing, and in South Los Angeles, where automotive and steel plants were folding.

"When he was in Long Beach, Pepsi and 7-Up and Kool cigarettes and Marlboro would come and set up a special display in the store and give him free cases of the stuff to sell," Maddox said. "If you're a small businessman and someone gives you 10, 15, 20 cases of 7-Up or Pepsi, just to put a display in, and you get to keep the money, that's a pretty good piece of change.

"When we decided to move back to South Los Angeles, my dad asked the delivery guy, 'Hey, you know those specials I used to get in Long Beach?' They said, 'We don't do that stuff down here.' "

There were symbols of resurgence, though, in South Los Angeles. One that stood out was the 394-bed Martin Luther King Jr. General Hospital, the first in the community, which opened in 1972.

Within three years, however, King Hospital became a symbol of neglect. As president of the hospital's house staff association, a young black physician named Louis Simpson led the interns and resident doctors on a strike against the county facility on the grounds that it was failing to meet the needs of people in the surrounding Watts and Compton areas. After a tense week during which 22 interns and residents were fired, the county caved in. The Board of Supervisors agreed to $5.5 million in improvements and hired the doctors back.

If there was any hope that this signaled renewed interest in the city's poor neighborhoods, the hope was short-lived. Faith in the system was evaporating. People felt Vietnam was symptomatic of a loss of national will. Watergate was evidence of a loss of integrity. Exposés of FBI and CIA crimes precipitated a loss of trust. Intractable problems of poverty and pollution further shook public confidence in the government. Economic growth stalled, but inflation soared. By the end of the decade, President Jimmy Carter was lamenting the nation's "malaise."

In South Los Angeles, Simpson saw more shootings. By the late '70s, Los Angeles' network of Crips and Bloods had taken shape, and the ritual slaughter accelerated. Gangs in Los Angeles County were killing nearly 300 rivals and bystanders a year, surpassing the number of gang-related deaths in Chicago and New York. And as tension on the streets rose, officer-involved shootings began to climb. Daryl F. Gates replaced Ed Davis as chief of the LAPD in 1978, pledging to restore its national standing.

His pledge almost immediately was challenged. Two LAPD officers shot and killed Eulia Love, a 39-year-old black woman, during a violent confrontation triggered by an unpaid gas bill. Police said Love brandished a kitchen knife when they came to investigate a reported assault on a meter reader. Two officers emptied their revolvers into her.

While the words "Crip" and "Blood" were setting families on edge in South Los Angeles during the late 1970s, white neighborhoods were up in arms about busing.

In 1963, the American Civil Liberties Union and the National Assn. for the Advancement of Colored People had filed a lawsuit to integrate Los Angeles public schools. But not until Sept. 12, 1978, were Latino, black, Asian and white students scheduled to trade seats.

JUNE 6, 1978

By a 65%-35% margin, California voters approve Proposition 13, the landmark state constitutional amendment that cut property taxes by two-thirds and made it harder to raise local taxes.

"You knew what to expect from
the lines were. In L.A., you don't

Though it affected only about 10% of all students in the school system, the integration program was still one of the largest ever attempted: 1,200 buses moving 64,000 fourth- through eighth-graders among 260 schools. Some white parents boycotted the schools in protest, keeping an estimated 10,000 children home the first day. In the San Fernando Valley, thousands of parents placed their children in hastily arranged private schools and tutoring programs.

Sitting in one of the new yellow buses as it chugged up to Sunny Brae Elementary School in Granada Hills was a black fifth-grader named Marcus, the son of a middle-class family in the Crenshaw District. "The first year we were bused, they protested us," recalled Marcus, who asked that only his first name be used. "There would be a big crowd outside the school and TV cameras. It was a big deal....

"Nobody ever called me a nigger or anything like that, but you knew they didn't want you out there."

White parents were less worried about black students being bused into their neighborhoods than about their own children being bused out. In 1979, a year after busing began, California voters approved a constitutional amendment forbidding state courts to order involuntary busing in desegregation cases. A state appeals court upheld the legality of the busing ban in 1980, and the Los Angeles Board of Education retired mandatory busing in 1981.

Distracted by the bitter black-and-white busing issue, many people in Los Angeles were only dimly aware of a new dynamic dramatically reordering the city's ethnic mix. Los Angeles—born a Latino city in 1776, when European immigrants on the East Coast were breaking away from Great Britain—was on the verge of being *reborn* as a Latino city in the 1980s.

Civil wars in Central America and a collapsing economy in Mexico were driving a new wave of immigrants to Los Angeles, one big enough to make an instant and undeniable impact on a city that might have believed itself accustomed to newcomers. In the 1980s, a time of unmatched growth, the county added 1.4 million residents. Nearly 1.3 million of them—92.9%—were Latino. Outnumbered 8-1 by Anglos in 1960, Latinos were nearly on par by 1990.

Sizable influxes of many other ethnic groups—Koreans and Russians, Vietnamese and Iranians—were hardly visible in the Latinos' shadow.

Although the new Latino immigrants were no more homogenous in their politics, their culture or their nature than the Anglo plurality, their sheer number altered the sprawling Los Angeles region from end to end. In particular, they were remaking the black core of South-Central.

One could begin to comprehend the transformation by visiting a sagging bungalow court on Florence Avenue near Figueroa Street. It had cheated fate a generation before, when much of the neighborhood was bulldozed to make room for the Harbor Freeway. By the '80s, the bungalows—now surrounded by a Burger King restaurant, four bullet-proofed gas stations and a mini-mall—had become representative of the new South L.A. They were home mostly to poor, working Latinas with small children. The courtyard was a good place to barbecue or let the children play in safety. Mothers looked after each other's kids. If one woman fell on

OCTOBER 15, 1979

Reformist junior officers launch a coup in El Salvador. More than a decade of civil war follows, launching an exodus of an estimated 300,000 refugees to Los Angeles.

white people in Mississippi. You knew what know where the lines are." —Laura Price, South Los Angeles resident since 1965

bad times, the others pitched in for food.

Leticia arrived, illegally, in 1988. She had boarded a bus in her native Mexico City three days earlier and journeyed north to move into the apartment of her friend, Anna, who had come to the United States in 1976 and worked in a beauty shop. The other women in the bungalow court worked in garment factories, or as maids, housekeepers and nannies, taking care of more affluent people's children. Whatever they saved went to family back in Mexico or Central America. "We have to live here because we can't live anywhere else," explained Anna, who, like Leticia, did not want her last name used.

Their apartment on one side looked out on the mini-mall, whose tenants included the Liquor Market, owned by William Hong, and a doughnut shop with no name. Hong had made a far different journey to this intersection in South-Central Los Angeles. He had left South Korea in 1981, when he was 24. In L.A., his first job was as a janitor in a restaurant. With his savings and the help of family and friends, he eventually started a hamburger stand at 3rd Street and Fairfax Avenue. Like his fellow Korean merchants, Hong saw poor neighborhoods as a business opportunity. Among the thousands of Koreans emigrating to the city, common wisdom said South Los Angeles, with its relatively low rents, was the best place to get a fast return on your dollar. But by the time he opened the liquor store at Florence and Figueroa, his illusions about America had evaporated. "I thought if you work hard, 14 hours a day, you can make your dreams come true," Hong said. "That's what I expected. Now, I see you have to be satisfied with just making a living."

For the public sector, the arrival of so many immigrants posed unprecedented challenges, as demands for health services soared and public schools scrambled to find more classroom space. Los Angeles schools groaned, in a decade adding 100,000 children speaking dozens of tongues. Making matters worse, all this happened in the years immediately after the Proposition 13 tax revolt, when government finances in California were strained as never before.

For private business, meanwhile, the new immigrants meant new consumers, renters and home buyers—and a huge reservoir of low-end wage earners to work in factories and shops.

The city's rich new ethnic mix was celebrated during the 1984 Summer Olympics—a refreshing triumph that contributed to a renaissance of American self-confidence and vaulted businessman Peter V. Ueberroth into the pantheon of popular heroes. Los Angeles' diversity was underscored in 1987, when Pope John Paul II celebrated multiethnic Masses at the Coliseum and Dodger Stadium.

Friction, however, was building. Blacks wondered how Koreans could come to this country and in no time find the capital to start their own businesses. They could find one answer in the story of Myung Lee, who owned the no-name doughnut shop next to Hong's liquor store.

Lee had come to Los Angeles in 1980. The winters were temperate, not like the bitterly cold winters in Seoul. In Los Angeles, she could escape the rigid social norms of her country. There weren't too many opportunities for a 37-year-old single woman in South Korea. "I liked the freedom," Lee said. "In this country, I could have dreams. I could be a woman, on my own, and make some money."

Starting on the graveyard shift at a South-Central gas station, where she risked her life for minimum wage, Lee worked hard and saved carefully. In 1989, after legalizing her status in the United States, she used $40,000 of her savings and a loan from an aunt to open the doughnut shop.

Lee's business seemed to be a sure bet. Indeed, in Southern California in the '80s, every business seemed a sure bet. Elected president in 1981, Ronald Reagan dramatically altered the national priorities and the public's mind-set—and rewrote the economy's rule book. Old-fashioned government aid for cities dwindled. But billions of dollars flowed into the Southland through an industrial base of enviable diversity. A junk-bond dealer from Encino named Michael Milken made $550 million in salary and bonuses in one year, 1987. Entire cities were born in the Inland Empire. Where once only wild grass grew after winter rains, men and women hit the road before sun-up to reach jobs close to the coast.

Somehow, the boom skipped South Los Angeles. As in the rest of the country, the gap between rich and poor widened. While black-owned stores faded, Korean-owned businesses seemed to dot every shopping area. Jobs seemed to be going to other people. Their very neighborhoods, blacks saw, were being transformed into the West Coast's fastest-growing Latino barrio. By the end of the '80s, Watts—a name synonymous with black Los Angeles—would become almost 50% Latino and begin holding Cinco de Mayo parades.

Marcus's friend Cletus, a member of the Compton Crip gang who claimed to have killed a man, lived in an area near Rodeo Road and Martin Luther King Jr. Boulevard called "The Jungle." After being kicked out of Dorsey High School for fighting and dropping out of another school, Cletus, who also asked that his last name not be used, earned a general-equivalency degree. Urged on by his mother, he enrolled in a computer training school in Hollywood, attending on a $3,000 federal loan that he was to repay once he landed a computer job with the help of the school. It was his tiny chunk of the billions of dollars in aid that poured into black Los Angeles in the 20-odd years following the Watts riots. Cletus graduated, but could not find a job. Businesses told him he needed two or three years of job experience.

A friend tipped him to a job at a computer company where he worked, so Cletus took the test along with four whites who applied. According to the friend—who graded the tests—Cletus scored higher than the white applicant whom the company actually hired. With a family to feed, Cletus took a job as a $6-an-hour security guard. "This is about the only kind of job you can get. I'm supposed to be making more money than this, and I would if I was doing computer work, but I've got a wife and two kids. I've got to do something. I still owe the government $3,000."

Steve Frank found one path to the good life: the Simi Valley Freeway. Like thousands of San Fernando Valley residents, Frank quit the city and moved his family to eastern Ventura County. By 1990, 250,000 people lived in the area, a

JUNE, 1983

A poll by the Urban Institute finds that about 70% of Southern Californians believe the influx of illegal immigrants has an unfavorable effect on the state. In Los Angeles County, almost 60% of blacks say illegal immigrants are taking jobs away from legal residents; only a minority of whites agrees.

1,786% increase since 1960. More than 80% of the residents were white. "We could see the gangs coming," said Frank, a public affairs consultant. "And the area had become so dirty. Not the air. The smog didn't bother me. It was the graffiti. And the Valley was the *best* part of L.A. It was pathetic." In Simi Valley, the Franks found sanctuary. With its low crime rate and good schools, Simi Valley was like the San Fernando Valley 30 years earlier. For $320,000, they bought a three-bedroom home with a large back yard. Steve's wife, Leslie, got a job as an elementary school principal and played the organ at the United Methodist Church.

Forty miles to the south, Nettie Lewis and her family were living on East 89th Street, a war zone. Lewis hated to see darkness come because at night there were so many shootings. One day, she dove to her kitchen floor when someone opened fire from the back of her house. The danger came not only from guns. Lewis' grandchildren, who lived with her, and their friends were accosted by older kids with knives. "Hey, I like your new shoes," junior high toughs taunted youngsters like her 11-year-old grandson, Derrell. "Give them to me or I'll cut you!" One 6-year-old gangbanger bragged to Derrell about owning a small pistol.

Years earlier, Lewis had felt safe enough to take evening strolls. Her daughters rode their bicycles from Watts to the beach or to drive-in movies. When the Santa Ana winds came, neighbors would stay outside long after dark to escape their stuffy houses. Neighborhood children would run to the schoolyard to shoot baskets or play flag football after school and on weekends. Few walls and houses seemed marred by graffiti.

The 1980s brought fewer jobs, but plenty of drugs and crime to Lewis' neighborhood. There was little money to spend, but prices stubbornly spiraled upward. Bicycle trips were limited to the neighborhood. Children were shooed inside before nightfall, followed closely by parents and grandparents. Schoolyards were now chained shut after hours. Parks belonged to gangbangers. Taggers were everywhere.

For Onamia Bryant, teaching became more than opening up textbooks and chalking lessons on a board. She saw the rising unemployment, the entrenched poverty, the drug culture reflected in her students. She became their surrogate mother, father, counselor and disciplinarian. A fellow teacher once told her a story that sticks in her mind. The teacher asked a little boy what he wanted to be when he grew up. "I'm going to be in jail," he said. "Why?" the teacher asked. "My daddy's in jail, and he's fine." To the little boy, to live in jail was safer than to try and survive on the streets. It was the place to be, like daddy.

For immigrant parents such as Basiliso Merino, living in South Los Angeles meant facing a grim reality. Low-flying police helicopters rattled the crowded, three-bedroom stucco house on Denver Avenue that his family shared with his brother, nephews and another family. The streets were often barricaded during drug sweeps. He had hoped his three daughters would get a good education, that they would learn English and start careers. But at the local public school, Bethune Junior High, the children learned that some of their fellow students carried guns and knives. After a year in school, the girls had learned hardly any English.

This was not the dream that drew Merino to Los Angeles. An accountant in Cuautitlán, a small town north of Mexico City, he had come north after an uncle

FEBRUARY 6, 1985

Police Chief Daryl F. Gates rides aboard the LAPD battering ram as it knocks a hole in the wall of a suspected Pacoima rock house. Officers find less than one-tenth of a gram of cocaine, and the district attorney's office refuses to file charges.

JUNE 4, 1985

Michael Woo becomes the first Asian-American to be elected to the City Council.

told him he had a job as a roofer at $50 a day. Merino took a note pad and made the calculation: 150,000 pesos. "I thought, 'That's a lot of money,' " he said. "I could never make that much in Mexico." But the pay proved to be an illusion. Taxes were taken out of his checks, and the work was not steady.

No one had to tell Nettie Lewis, Onamia Bryant or Basiliso Merino the statistics, but they were there, compiled by government agencies, if anyone wondered. In 1990, one of every five of the Los Angeles Unified School District's students lived in poverty. One-third of all pupils lived in families with no health insurance. Many had never seen a physician before they began their schooling. Sixty percent of the students were scoring below average in basic skills proficiency.

At the Augustus Hawkins Mental Health Clinic in Watts, Louis Simpson watched the casualties roll into his outpatient clinic: the child gangsters, the crack dealers, the killers, the broken families, the dispirited and the overwhelmed. We are all victims, the psychiatrist told them. Crips and Bloods? Like Italian and Irish gangsters before them, these black youths, he believed, simply were using criminal means to achieve the American dream because all other paths were blocked.

But the L.A. street gangs had something the earlier gangs did not—crack cocaine. It arrived in Los Angeles' poor areas in the early '80s. While the city basked in the glow of the Olympic Games, cocaine powder was refined to the cheaper, more addictive crack. Like no other drug, crack devastated families, sucking thousands of dollars out of modest households. Fred Williams saw it whenever he took walks through the Jordan Downs housing project. As a teaching assistant at the local elementary school, his job was to coax parents into sending their children to class. He would find a stray child and take him home, only to find the parents cutting up dope on the kitchen table. It's crazy! he thought.

Williams had been raised better than this, in a tough neighborhood but in a single-family home, by a mother who paid attention. With that strength behind you, you could go wrong—as he had, dealing cocaine out of Denker Park near the Coliseum with his buddies in the Harlem 30s Crips—but you still have a chance to make it. Here, the odds were preposterous. You could see the Marvin Gaye line: *This ain't living*. Williams got a barber's clippers and began giving some of the young boys haircuts. There were boys, 6 and 7 years old, who'd never had their hair cut. They were cute now, he thought, but in a few years that cuteness would be gone.

Williams ran into a teen-ager named Darren on the stoop of one of the project's apartments. Darren had been out of school two years—just hadn't gone. He had promised Williams he would go back.

"What's up?" Williams asked softly.

"I didn't get no clothes for Easter," the boy said.

"So what?"

"Mother had to pay her bills."

"You gotta keep washing your clothes by hand, Darren. There some things you're going to have to deal with. You have to get used to getting up and taking care of business."

Gang violence in the city seemed to spread by the day. No one was

OCTOBER 17, 1986

Congress approves the Immigration Reform and Control Act, creating an amnesty program for illegal immigrants and barring employment of illegals who do not qualify.

untouchable, not sad-eyed old people, not cool teen-agers, not cooing babies. But it wasn't until a summer night in 1988 that white people really took notice. A young Asian-American woman named Karen Toshima was shot and killed by gang cross-fire that erupted in Westwood Village—a place ostensibly safe from inner-city terror. The murder shocked the affluent Westside. City leaders demanded that Chief Gates and the LAPD prevent it from ever happening again.

Operation Hammer was born. In a series of unprecedented sweeps, the police rounded up thousands of black men and other people they suspected of being gang members or drug dealers, accused them of petty crimes and temporarily locked them up.

Simmering complaints about police brutality erupted into public controversies. On Aug. 1, 1988, a force of 80 LAPD officers stormed two apartment buildings near 39th Street and Dalton Avenue, ransacking the homes and beating the residents. On Jan. 14, 1989, in a "sting," an NBC News camera crew videotaped Long Beach police officers apparently pushing Don Jackson—a black Hawthorne police sergeant on administrative leave—through a storefront window. On Jan. 23, 1990, Los Angeles County Sheriff's deputies shot and killed a 27-year-old black Muslim named Oliver R. Beasley following a traffic stop. Beasley's killing, later ruled justifiable by both the district attorney's office and a Norwalk Superior Court civil jury, drew national attention when Muslim leader Louis Farrakhan called it "murder" before a crowd of 16,000 at a Sports Arena rally following the young man's funeral.

As a police liaison to Mayor Bradley in the mid-1980s, Kerman Maddox listened to plenty of citizen complaints. Before that, when Eulia Love was killed by police, Maddox marched. During a controversy over police chokeholds, when Chief Gates said the arteries of some blacks were not like those of "normal" people, Maddox again took to the streets.

One night in November of 1988, he noticed a police car pulling in behind him as he returned to his La Salle Avenue home. Maddox, a Neighborhood Watch leader, went over to see what was up. An argument ensued. Maddox said he was cursed, kicked and beaten by the officers. He filed a complaint, but the officers were cleared by the LAPD internal affairs department. Maddox got a lawyer and won an out-of-court settlement with the city.

Still, even Maddox was unprepared for the image on his TV screen on March 4, 1991.

FEBRUARY 19, 1991

City Councilwoman Gloria Molina, a laborer's daughter, is elected to the Los Angeles County Board of Supervisors, the first Latino and the first woman elected to the five-member board.

MAR. 3 1991

Millions of people around the world saw the videotape of Rodney G. King being severely beaten by four Los Angeles police officers. The beating created a nationwide furor over police brutality.

From George Holliday video/ via KTLA-TV

THE PATH TO FURY

3

Surrounded by a clutch of police officers in the glare of patrol car headlights, a large man rises from the ground and lurches in the direction of a baton-wielding cop. The officer swings once, catching the man in the upper body and dropping him face-first to the pavement. Then he steps forward to hammer the man again and again.

Another officer joins the fray, swinging his own metal baton and repeatedly kicking the man writhing on the ground. A third officer enters the semicircle of blue uniforms and administers what appears to be yet another kick. Seconds creep like hours as the batons continue to swing, 56 times in all.

"Oh, my God, they're beating him to death!" a horrified woman wails from her balcony in a nearby apartment building. "What are they going to do, kill him?"

Her cry isn't registered by the hand-held video camera used by plumber George Holliday to capture the assault on tape, but millions of television viewers who watch the images repeatedly in coming weeks will share the thought.

Once seen, the TV footage of the beating of Rodney King is difficult to forget. The violence is harsh, brutal, savage. Almost as chilling is what the camera doesn't capture—the message that one of the baton-swinging officers, Laurence M. Powell, sent to another officer minutes before the episode in Lake View Terrace. The words seem to confirm the community's most serious qualms about its Police Department's worst members. Before confronting King, Powell had likened a black family's domestic dispute to "Gorillas in the Mist." After King was subdued, some witnesses said the arresting officers bragged of their violence and taunted their victim.

Dr. Edmund Chein, one of five emergency room physicians who tended to King immediately after the beating, said the officers' baton strokes were so violent they literally knocked the fillings out of some of King's teeth. One of King's eye sockets was shattered, a cheekbone was fractured, a leg broken. His flesh was bruised by the repeated blows. A concussion and painful facial nerve damage complicated his other injuries.

The incident began soon after midnight, March 3, 1991, when King, a 25-year-old high school dropout and part-time Dodger Stadium groundskeeper from Altadena, passed a California Highway Patrol car on the Foothill Freeway in Sun Valley. King was out with a couple of friends for a night of driving, talking and drinking. The CHP cruiser pulled behind his white 1988 Hyundai and flashed its red lights. King, who was on parole for a second-degree robbery conviction, panicked and sped up. After he exited the freeway, LAPD units joined the chase.

When King finally did stop, near a large apartment complex, more than two dozen law enforcement officers—21 from the LAPD, four from the CHP and two from the Los Angeles Unified School District—converged on his car. Police later said that King, following an officer's orders, emerged from his Hyundai and lay on the ground. Powell sought to handcuff the prone man, police said, but King flung Powell and other officers away.

"That's when the fight started," said Richard Talkington, the LAPD traffic detective who initially investigated the incident.

Most witnesses in the apartment building said King was calm, complying with the officers' orders to get out of the car and lie on the ground. They said police hit him in the chest with a Taser stun gun as he lay on his back, then clubbed him without provocation. One CHP officer at the scene said that King appeared amused by the small army of officers, not combative. His most threatening gesture, she said, was to grab his buttocks while parading in front of them. She thought he was drunk but not dangerous.

Los Angeles police, however, insisted that King *was* dangerous. That he reached in a pocket, as if he were armed, when he stepped from his car. That he ignored orders to lie still on the ground. That he seemed to be on PCP, a powerful drug that can spur reckless aggression in people—though tests found no evidence of the drug in King's system.

King himself had a fuzzy memory of the event. He conceded that he and his friends had been drinking malt liquor and that he had run from the CHP to try to dodge a ticket. But he said he never would have been fool enough to resist arrest, especially while surrounded by so many armed officers.

The portrait of a lone man blindly attacking a platoon of police certainly did not fit the Rodney King his friends knew. King's 6-foot-3, 225-pound frame could intimidate some people, they acknowledged, but behind the bulk was a passive, gentle human being. A "Baby Huey," one friend said.

This Baby Huey had spent time in prison, however. In November, 1989, King had threatened a Monterey Park grocer with a tire iron and robbed him of $200. But the grocer, Tae Suck Baik, said that *he* was the aggressor, whipping King with a rod kept near the cash register. King then hit him once and fled with the money. King drove away from Baik's 99 Market in his own car, which police easily traced. The grocer later said he felt sorry for King.

Friends said the robbery was the foolish impulse of a learning-disabled, unemployed man desperate to provide for his wife and two young sons. While serving a year in the Susanville, Calif., work camp, King wrote to a judge to acknowledge his error and apologize. Paroled two days after Christmas, 1990, he was scheduled to start a permanent job as a construction worker the day after he was beaten and arrested.

Some of the four officers later charged with beating King also seemed unlikely candidates for a confrontation. Powell, 28, was raised in a house filled with foster children of all races. Timothy E. Wind, 30, had only recently signed up with the LAPD after seven unremarkable years as a cop in a suburb of Kansas City, Mo. Veteran Sgt. Stacey C. Koon, 40, had used mouth-to-mouth resuscitation to try to save the life of an AIDS-infected black transvestite prostitute. The fourth officer, Theodore J. Briseno, 38, had a history of using excessive force. But he was the least involved of the four.

Still, reaction to the tape was swift and sharp. The grainy video images of police beating a prone and pleading man were powerful enough to yank the nation's attention from the grainy video images of guided missiles smashing Iraq in the just-concluded Gulf War.

Mayor Tom Bradley, himself a former LAPD officer, was "shocked and outraged" and promised a swift prosecution of the officers involved. "This is something which we cannot and will not tolerate," he said. Even other police professionals were unnerved by the ferocity of the beating. Dallas Police Chief William Rathburn, a former assistant chief of the LAPD, called it "gross criminal misconduct." LAPD Officer Tom Sullivan, expressing the shame and anger of many cops, said, "This isn't just a case of excessive force. It's a case of mass stupidity."

Regular citizens started giving cops dirty looks, making obscene gestures. And this was in the Valley, on the Westside, where police thought they could count on support. A Los Angeles Times Poll in the week after the beating found that 92% of Angelenos believed the police used excessive force against King. Two-thirds thought police brutality was common.

Yale University law professor Drew Days, a former assistant U.S. attorney general, echoed a common thought: "It is astounding that anybody could look at that film and not conclude that those police officers were violating someone's civil rights."

Los Angeles Police Chief Daryl F. Gates later would say that the first time he saw the tape it made him "physically ill." Immediately after the assault, he refrained from criticizing his officers. But four days later, Gates said the four should be charged with felony assault. His beloved LAPD already was reeling from the mindlessly destructive raid at 39th Street and Dalton Avenue, a mounting pile of controversial shootings and the vexing ineffectiveness of get-tough gang programs like Operation Hammer.

Now this ugly little videotape—maddeningly, it was being shown on more stations more often than "Dragnet" reruns—was threatening to put the department down for the count.

A rt Washington was as horrified as the rest of the city when the tape rolled at the top of the evening newscast. But after the initial reaction—revulsion, anger, sympathy—he started to wonder if some good might not come of it. "Well, at last they *see* we're not lying to them," he thought. "They see that this stuff actually happens. Now the *world* sees. They always think we're making it up."

A member of the city's black middle class, he had a real stake in the system. His pesticide business—opened 15 years earlier, when he worked as a molding-machine operator—was prospering. He had started by going door to door in South Los Angeles, asking people if they had ants or roaches; now two new computers tallied the accounts of 7,000 customers.

The tape grabbed Steve Frank's attention in Simi Valley. "When you look

at the videotape, without knowing any more, you think these guys should be shot," he said. But you never know.

For Washington's nephew, UCLA student Tim Howell Jr., the videotape was an education. Your parents can tell you all the stories in the world about what some police do to black people, but until you see it you don't understand. "I was messed up when I saw it," he said.

It reinforced the constant tension of being a Young Black Male, the embodiment of the nation's most negative stereotype. Howell was dating a young woman from Windsor Hills, one of those fashionable white communities that became a fashionable black community after the Watts riot. Unlike his father, who preferred staying close to home and his latest enterprise, baking cakes, the younger Howell roamed the city. And yet he felt its racial creases, the places where he was plainly uncomfortable, without a word spoken. Sometimes he would go to dinner with his girlfriend and her parents to a nice restaurant, and he could feel the stares when they walked in: What are *they* doing here?

Los Angeles at the time was in one of its cranky winter moods, an angry attitude made worse because the sky spits rain in your eye but won't ease the drought. Lazy days at the beach were a memory, traffic inched slower than usual. The recession that came for a visit had decided to stay. Despite the Gulf War— *another* knot in the city's stomach—thousands of pink slips were out looking for defense workers.

The first weekend after the King beating, hundreds of youths tore up Westwood Village. Some looted stores and vandalized cars, angry after ticket buyers were turned away from "New Jack City," a film about a Harlem drug lord. "Fight the power!" the angry crowd yelled, cribbing the title of a popular rap song. Others made angry references to the King beating.

A week later, the four officers were booked, arraigned and freed on bail. "The conduct of those officers on that scene that night is the most reprehensible thing that I've seen occur in this city," Mayor Bradley said. "And I think that we are on the road to bringing to justice those who committed the illegal acts." The

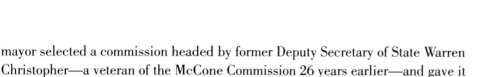

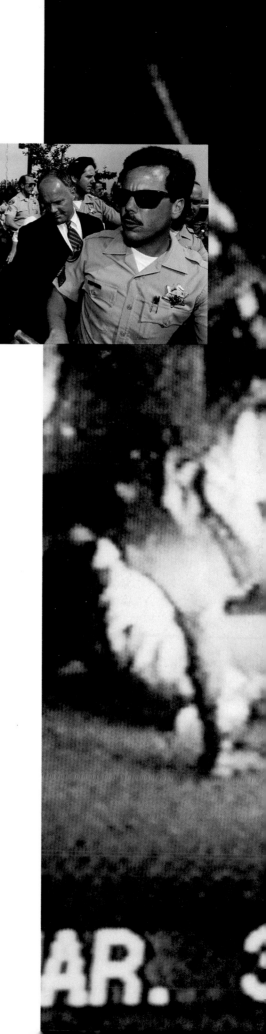

mayor selected a commission headed by former Deputy Secretary of State Warren Christopher—a veteran of the McCone Commission 26 years earlier—and gave it 100 days to investigate the Police Department and recommend reforms.

Bradley counseled patience, but he had little himself for Gates. Although he refrained from publicly asking for the chief's resignation, the mayor privately blamed Gates for the hardened attitudes that he believed led to the beating. His staff tried to orchestrate the ouster of Gates behind the scenes. Within a week, however, the word was out that Police Commission Vice President Melanie Lomax had asked the city attorney's office how to discipline or fire the chief.

At the time, a Los Angeles Times Poll found that only 31% of the city's residents wanted to be rid of Gates. News of the Police Commission's action pushed dithering City Council members off the fence and into the chief's camp. When the Police Commission, appointed by Bradley, put Gates on leave, the City Council reinstated him the following day. Lomax later leaked the city attorney's advice on disciplining Gates to a civil rights group trying to force him out of office, sparking another uproar. Gates and Bradley severed all contact; they would not speak to one another again until the city was aflame a year later. City government was splintering as fast as Los Angeles itself.

Toward the end of March, as the Battle of City Hall was heating up, racial tension in South-Central jumped off the scale. A black teen-ager named Latasha Harlins walked into the Empire Liquor Market Deli on South Figueroa Street for some orange juice. After a fight with Korean-born storekeeper Soon Ja Du over whether the 15-year-old had tried to steal the juice, Harlins put the bottle on the counter and turned to leave. Du shot her in the back of the head.

A video camera—a store security camera—recorded it all. Weeks later, a black man named Lee Arthur Mitchell tried to buy a wine cooler at Chung's Liquor Market near Western Avenue and 79th Street, offering some jewelry as a partial payment. When the owner's wife refused, Mitchell, his hand in his pocket, pretended to point a handgun at her and ordered the cash register emptied. The owner, Tae Sam Park, produced a real gun. A struggle ensued and

Ethnic tensions flared in 1991 after Korean-born grocer Soon Ja Du, below, shot and killed 15-year-old Latasha Harlins after a scuffle over orange juice in Du's Empire Liquor Market Deli on South Figueroa Street.

Photo: Ken Lubas

Mitchell was mortally wounded in the chest.

The district attorney's office filed charges against Du, but concluded that Park's actions were justified. Many black residents concluded otherwise. Daily picketing of Park's grocery began, coordinated by the Brotherhood Crusade. One day, a young black gang member walked into the store and asked for a bottle of malt liquor and two cans of baby food. He watched Kum Ock Park ring up the items and then told her to cancel the sale.

"The next time you want to sell this," he said, his speech punctuated with obscenities, "think about the [person] you killed." Ultimately, Park's store was closed as part of a black-Korean agreement brokered by Mayor Bradley.

A mile away from Soon Ja Du's liquor store, at the Florence Avenue mini-mall where they operated two shops, Myung Lee and William Hong felt the angry vibrations.

"Sometimes, you feel kind of scared," Hong said. "Especially at night. No one ever did anything violent to me. But you still feel this fear."

Lee learned a few words of Spanish to communicate better with Latinos, who made up three-fourths of her clientele. She gave free coffee and doughnuts to police officers, who made her no-name doughnut shop a law enforcement hangout. A gunman once stole her purse, but all in all she felt fortunate. She knew her customers, and they knew her.

The world surrounding these people was becoming increasingly inhospitable. This recession was wiping out white-collar jobs, not just industrial ones. Their tax bases depleted, Mayor Bradley, Gov. Pete Wilson and Los Angeles school district officials were planning large budget cuts that would result in fewer teachers, lower payments to mothers with dependent children and less after-school child care at school campuses. The city was paying record sums to settle excessive force cases against the police; by year's end, the total would exceed $13 million. Members of street gangs were killing each other—and innocent neighborhood residents—at nearly double the rate of a few years earlier.

In July, the Christopher Commission explained the soaring civil penalties against police by criticizing LAPD leadership for tolerating undisciplined officers and racism-tinged behavior. Supervising officers, aware of abuse by their personnel, did little to stop it, the commission concluded in its 228-page report. Use of excessive force and racially motivated brutality were tolerated, and that tolerance seemed to be institutionalized.

Looking for a way to shore up the LAPD's crumbling credibility, the commission recommended that civilian authorities reassert control over the department and suggested that Gates and the police commissioners who unsuccessfully sought to remove him should step down. It called for revising the City Charter to limit the term of the police chief and make the chief more accountable to elected officials and the public.

Only two Police Commission members—Lomax and Sam Williams—offered to quit. Gates defiantly refused to retire, taking the offensive instead. On a day his critics wanted him to resign, the chief told 100 chanting supporters that he would stay in office and stay the course. "This Police Department is aggressive," he said. "We're going to use all the means at our disposal that we can to bring down the crime and violence."

Without mentioning Gates, Bradley shot back: "I say to those who would block the road to change: Stand aside or we will leave you behind." The City Council and Bradley put the Christopher Commission reforms on the June, 1992, ballot; Gates, whose retirement plans would shift repeatedly, indicated at this point that he would step down only if voters approved the changes.

The bombast was sapping the confidence of the department's foot soldiers, its 4,300 patrol officers. Some began to see parallels with the Vietnam War: The LAPD marshaled its resources like a military juggernaut, they said, but the command structure was impotent because it was politicized. "The LAPD in 1991 is the American military in 1968," said one ranking officer. "We used our big guns, and now it's fallen apart. The command is bickering. The program's rudderless. A lot of people on the street took Gates seriously when he said we could win against crime. Not everyone, but a lot of us. Well, you can't tell anyone anymore that this is a winnable war."

Faced with all the confusion, some cops started hanging back until the department's future became clearer—cruising past the minor violations, the crack transactions, the motel prostitutes and alley dice games. "We're not sweating the small stuff," a Southeast Division patrolman said. It showed. Arrests for nonviolent crimes fell by 34,300—a drop of more than 20%—in the first nine months of 1991. Publicly, the brass declined to jump to conclusions. But there were no illusions among the rank and file.

Illusions were dying all over the city that summer. Jake Flukers' died when General Motors said it would close its Van Nuys plant. Despite years of community pleas and union compromises, Flukers and his 2,600 colleagues were told they had one year before their jobs moved to Canada without them. Thousands more skilled workers were made redundant elsewhere in the county, as federal officials answered the Soviet Union's collapse by trimming defense spending.

Pollution, congestion, the cost of living and the cost of doing business—all the headaches of a mature industrial economy—were pushing employers to think about leaving the Southland. The shift had begun in 1987—the first year since 1971's aerospace bust in which manufacturing employment in Los Angeles declined—but it was getting worse. Orange County in 1991 saw its first decline in manufacturing jobs in 40 years.

Crime was encouraging the exodus—and leading to increasingly violent conflicts between minority residents and police.

Arturo Jimenez, an East Los Angeles gang member, was shot dead by a sheriff's deputy in a housing project on Aug. 3. Sheriff's officials said that Jimenez had grabbed another deputy's flashlight and knocked the officer unconscious. Residents, after facing officers in a tense standoff, said Jimenez simply argued with deputies and never struck anyone.

Three more controversial fatal shootings by sheriff's deputies followed in the next month. In Ladera Heights on Aug. 13, a mentally disturbed man was shot eight times in the back and once in the shoulder. In Artesia on Aug. 28, a 15-year-old boy was killed. In Willowbrook Park on Sept. 2, another man died. The district attorney's office took the shootings to the grand jury, seeking criminal charges against the five deputies involved.

Sheriff Sherman Block responded on Sept. 10 by naming his own panel of community leaders to recommend reforms. Critics sneered that Block was merely seeking to stall a truly independent investigation.

In September, Fred Williams took a job as a "dropout retrieval" specialist with the Compton Unified School District. By now he was something of a local hero. His willingness to walk into dangerous communities and demand that parents pay more attention to their children's education had led to national television exposure. One of the first things he did in Compton was set up a meeting with 100 high-risk black and Latino students in an auditorium.

In the news that morning, Mayor Bradley proposed job training and classes in self-esteem at Williams' old stomping grounds, the Jordan Downs housing project. The week before, five Latino residents of the project had died in an arson fire that appeared to stem from a racial dispute with a group of blacks.

That was the level of disaster that it now took to get the government's attention, Williams figured. It was a reality that Williams wanted these kids to understand: In this society, you walk a tightrope, and there is no net, not for poor people. Look at the education they were getting here. Compton had the worst test scores in California. "If you expecting somebody to fall in love with you because you're young, you can forget it," he said. "Ain't nobody taking care of us at all. We got to come up with our own ways of taking care of business. If there's anything you remember after today, remember that.

"I was just like y'all. I was 14 and I shot a boy smooth in the middle of his head....I still see his family. And it hits me, you know what I'm saying? The s---- is *real*. Have any of y'all ever killed anybody? You got no idea how it feels. You got to understand, boy. You ever heard the old saying 'Count your blessings'? I'm telling you. Telling you...."

Two months later, on Nov. 15, 1991, Joyce Karlin did some telling. The Los Angeles Superior Court judge told a hushed courtroom, guarded by extraordinary security, that this was a time for healing, not revenge. She sentenced Soon Ja Du to five years' probation—and no time behind bars—for killing Latasha Harlins.

"Latasha's death," said the judge, "should be remembered as a catalyst, to force [blacks and Koreans] to confront an intolerable situation and ... create solutions."

It would not be.

If there was an award for pessimistic prescience on that day, it had to go to Diane Watson, the state senator representing South Los Angeles. "This," she said, "might be the time bomb that explodes."

So many bombs were ticking through 1991. Rodney King. Latasha Harlins. And Baby.

Baby is a cocker spaniel. On June 30, Glendale authorities arrested her 26-year-old owner, Brendan Sheen, for repeatedly kicking and jumping on the puppy, breaking her ribs and pelvis. Sheen, facing the possibility of three years in prison, pleaded guilty to felony animal cruelty. Five days after Soon Ja Du got probation for killing a teen-ager, Sheen got 30 days in jail.

"For beating a dog!" Art Washington exclaimed.

News accounts of Sheen's sentencing were not prominent, but in black communities the word filtered around. The symbolism was agonizing. "That's not justice for all," complained schoolteacher Onamia Bryant.

The confluence of the cases stirred not only outrage, but memories of prior indignities at the hands of law enforcement. So often, particularly for black men, the suffering involved a traffic stop—the same spark that had kindled the Watts riots. White people unlucky enough to be stopped by officers with guns drawn would remember a single incident with fear for years. Young black men considered it a frightening, degrading routine.

Marcus and Cletus had their memories. For Marcus, it was Torrance. He was driving a friend home. They were sitting in the car, talking, when a sheriff's black-and-white rolled up. "You know the routine," he said. "The thing that gets me is that they always say the same thing: 'We've been having a lot of robberies in this neighborhood and you look like the suspect.' "

Cletus recalled being stopped for running a stoplight when the brakes failed on his cousin's car. "They had us all out of the car, spread-eagle. They searched the car and everything. I told him what happened. He said, 'Well, you should have tried to stop sooner.' I told him that I wasn't familiar with the car. He was with this young Hispanic officer, and he told him, 'I'm going to show you how to get some practice.' Then he started cursing me out: 'I could take your ass to jail right now.' I started getting mad, then my friend said, 'If he's going to jail, then I'm going to jail.' He said he did that because he could see that the cop had a throwaway gun in his waistband. He figured they'd just go around the corner somewhere, shoot me and then plant a gun on me."

It wasn't just this war of nerves with police that strained life in South Los Angeles. It was the violence that imprisoned you and the high prices that impoverished you. By 1991, Nettie Lewis had lived on East 89th Street in South-Central for 22 years. While the complexion of the neighborhood had changed—whites were long gone, and most of the neighbors were Latino—the poverty endured and maltreatment lingered.

Her daughter said she purchased a large bag of potato chips in Inglewood for 79 cents and found the same bag cost $1.79 in Watts. If you didn't have a car, and many residents did not, you paid the going price.

Beatrice Johnson, Lewis' next-door neighbor, said many blacks resented the treatment they got in local stores, where owners—especially Koreans—followed them down the aisles, apparently worried that they were shoplifters. "It was

insulting. They were treating us with no respect, like we were thieves," she said.

Nine days after Brendan Sheen got 30 days for beating his dog,
Los Angeles police officers fatally shot a 28-year-old black man, Henry Peco, in
Watts' Imperial Courts housing project. They said he had ambushed them while
they investigated a power outage, a fact later confirmed by Peco's accomplices. But
the accomplices had carried off Peco's assault rifle, casting doubt on the official
story. A confrontation with more than 100 residents ensued.

S immering discontent over police shootings and the political free-for-all at City
Hall led Los Angeles Superior Court Judge Stanley Weisberg in November to
select Ventura County as the site of the trial of the four officers charged in the
Rodney King beating. A month later, the Los Angeles County Grand Jury
refused to bring criminal charges against sheriff's deputies in connection with
the four fatal summertime shootings.

Little of this was felt in the small apartment building on Florence Avenue
where Leticia and Anna lived. Politics was not their concern. Indeed, for many
Latino immigrants in South Los Angeles, the Rodney King affair stirred none
of the passions it inflamed in their black neighbors.

Latinos meshed better with the Korean store owners, too. The Latinos who
bought their milk and money orders at William Hong's liquor store liked him. They
called him "Chino," a generic term in Spanish-speaking Los Angeles for any Asian.
Chino is a good guy, he gives you credit, they would say. He kept the running tabs
on thin strips of paper tacked to the wall behind his cash register. You need some
milk for the baby? Don't have any cash? No problem—Chino will let you have it.
Hong even spoke a little Spanish, saying *gracias* to his customers.

For both blacks and Latinos, however, life in South Los Angeles steered a
new course after March 5, 1992, when the lawyers made their opening statements
in the Simi Valley trial of the officers accused of beating King.

Prosecutors repeatedly showed jurors the infamous videotape; defense
lawyers blamed the incident on King himself—and each other's clients. John
Barnett, Briseno's lawyer, said that the other officers were "out of control" and that
Briseno had merely tried to stop them.

Prosecutors spent two weeks presenting their case, calling emergency room
physicians and nurses to the witness stand to describe King's injuries and recount
how the officers bragged about inflicting them. Several other law enforcement
personnel, including the Highway Patrol officers who started the chase, condemned
the overwhelming use of force. One person not put on the stand was a man many
assumed would be the star prosecution witness—King himself.

Defense attorneys countered with witnesses—paramedics and other police
officers who were at the scene that night—who testified that the videotape did not
tell the whole story. It did not show King when he emerged from his car, when
police said he resisted their orders. It did not accurately portray where King was
struck with the police batons or how badly he really was injured. It did not show
how scared the ring of police officers was of the man they were trying to arrest.

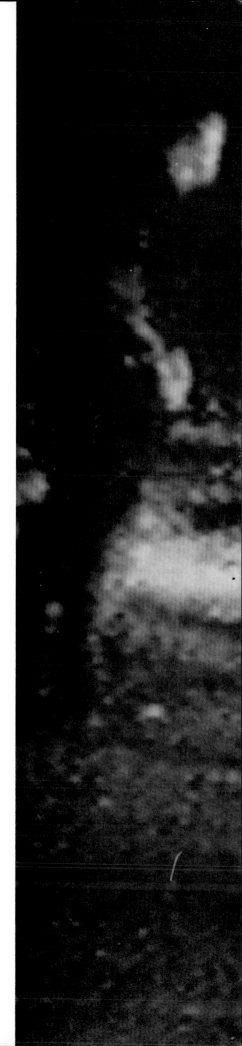

Jurors began their deliberations on Thursday, April 23. Chief Gates, in a videotaped speech broadcast to LAPD officers, urged "calm, maturity and professionalism" regardless of the verdict. Three days later, with jurors still closeted, the Rev. Cecil L. (Chip) Murray of the First African Methodist Episcopal Church—in a Sunday sermon to his politically influential congregation—urged the city's black community to "be cool, even in anger, be cool."

Temperatures, meanwhile, soared into the 90s. Life went on in Los Angeles; good things happened. A Lucky supermarket opened in the Baldwin Hills-Crenshaw Plaza, giving South Los Angeles its first new major grocery store since the 1965 Watts riots. But the city hardly noticed. Day by day by day, Los Angeles fixed its gaze on Simi Valley, waiting for the jury to make up its mind.

ABOVE
Though Police Chief Daryl F. Gates did not strongly condemn the King beating at the time of the incident, he reveals in his newly released autobiography that the videotape, which he says he reviewed 25 times the morning after the assault, made him feel "sick to my stomach, sick at heart."

Photo: Steve Dykes

At the beginning of the unrest, images would shock and sadden viewers nationwide, as had those of the videotaped beating of Rodney King a year earlier. As millions looked on, truck driver Reginald O. Denny was dragged from the cab of

"MY GOD, THIS IS IT."

4

WEDNESDAY, APRIL 29, 1992

At every watershed through time, a face emerges to transfix a moment in history. In Vietnam, a naked girl fled napalm. In Tian An Men Square, a single student stared down a line of Chinese tanks. In Los Angeles in 1991, Rodney King lay prone and beaten. And on the day the jury returned its verdicts on the four police officers in the King case, a new image burned its way into the public consciousness: a white truck driver dragged from his cab at a South Los Angeles intersection and beaten nearly into oblivion.

The brutal ambush, like the three days of rioting that followed, was recorded on videotape by television news helicopters hovering overhead—to be broadcast, like the earlier King tape, over and over and over for weeks before a horrified, onlooking world. There the man lay, an anonymous driver, beset by angry black men, knocked to the asphalt, beaten, kicked, bashed with a fire extinguisher and abandoned—after having his pockets picked.

Within days, his name would become almost as familiar as King's. The attack on Reginald Denny would become the flip side of the attack on King—the unofficial, black-on-white answer to the official, white-on-black beating. Within hours, Los Angeles would plummet into chaos.

Television and radio trumpeted the not-guilty verdicts from Courtroom Number 3 in Simi Valley. Mayor Bradley appeared at a press conference, saying he was stunned, shocked and outraged: "I was speechless when I heard that verdict. Today this jury told the world that what we saw with our own eyes is not a crime." Joseph Lowery, president of the Southern Christian Leadership Conference, expressed fear for the nation. Even in South Africa, he said, white police officers are punished for beating blacks. Benjamin Hooks, the executive director of the NAACP, called the verdicts outrageous: "Given the evidence, it is difficult to see how the jurors will ever live with their consciences."

The meaning of the verdicts, and the rationale behind them, would remain the subject of speculation—a source of self-congratulation for the defense, disappointment for the prosecution and rage among many who would soon hear the news.

Michael Stone, Officer Powell's lawyer, pronounced himself satisfied. The defense team had managed "to do what we set out to do"—to get the jurors to look at the case not through the eyes of an amateur video buff but "through the eyes of the police officers." Terry White, lead prosecutor on the case, shared the prevalent public reaction: shock. He was also bitterly disappointed. He still believed the evidence justified convicting the officers. But the jury had disagreed.

WEDNESDAY, APRIL 29, 4 P.M.
The Simi Valley Courthouse

It was chaotic. Ten not-guilty verdicts had sent scores of reporters scrambling in every direction, searching for jurors, defendants, prosecutors, attorneys and community activists.

The jury and most of the defendants didn't want to talk. Sgt. Stacey C. Koon was nearly tackled by a throng of reporters and cameramen as he tried to slip away unnoticed. "You're guilty! You're guilty!" protesters shouted at a tight-lipped Koon, as the advancing crowd crushed a photographer against a parked car.

Inside the courthouse, Officer Laurence M. Powell—accused of striking the most blows on Rodney G. King—stood grinning in a klieg-lit second-floor briefing room. "I am very happy, very happy," he declared.

In response to a question, Powell said he had nothing to say to those upset by the verdicts. "I don't think I have to respond to them," he said. "They have to respond to themselves and make their own decision. I don't think there is anything I can do to change their feelings."

DEAN E. MURPHY
Times staff writer

The change of venue, experts later would say, had handicapped the prosecution. It had produced a conservative jury predisposed to favor the police. What else could be expected, some asked, from a mostly white jury of suburbanites, of which eight had either served in the armed forces or had spouses who had been in the military?

King's lawyer, Steve Lerman, was furious with the verdicts. "It says it's OK to beat somebody on the ground and beat the crap out of him," he fumed. "There is nothing Rodney King did to deserve this fate, and the [officers] are walking out as heroes...."

If the verdicts were to be a test, people saw in it many different lessons. When Steve Frank of Simi Valley had first seen the King videotape 14 months earlier, he had thought the four officers should be shot. But watching the verdicts on television at home with his twin daughters, he found himself unwilling to second-guess the jury. That's why we have juries, reasoned the public affairs consultant, to sort out things we can't see on an 81-second videotape. Frank wasn't sure what those things were, but he was sure that the jurors were sure. He respected their decision.

Jake Flukers, on the other hand, could imagine no way a jury could find those people innocent. He had seen the whipping that man got. The tall, black union representative heard the news Wednesday afternoon as he was leaving the G.M. plant in Van Nuys. He went to phone his sons, ages 12 and 13, who lived with their mother in Lake View Terrace. If they had received the word, they would be furious. He wanted to talk them down. What do you feel like? Flukers asked the younger one.

"I feel like going to get a gun," the boy said.

"For what?" Flukers asked.

"To go kill all those white folks."

"You can't kill all white folks," Flukers said. "That boy you play basketball with, he's white."

Flukers went and picked up his boys. They stopped to buy sodas near the corner where King was beaten. Protesters were gathering. Flukers saw that the boys had to vent their rage. So he let them join the protesters, carrying signs, for a little while.

In South Los Angeles, 24-year-old Marcus had had enough. Raised in an inner-city home but bused to suburban schools, he could appreciate the impulse to put your faith in the system. But this was too much. The King beating was on videotape, Marcus knew. They had beaten the man senseless. They had mistakenly believed that he was on PCP, then one of them had joked about the beating. How could they not be guilty of *something*? It brewed inside him, the fury.

A few miles away, his friend Cletus had a similar reaction. These police, Cletus smoldered, they run around with badges and think they have a right to do anything to you. Cletus and Marcus decided to get their rage out, too. Somebody was going to pay.

As word spread, political recriminations began. The verdicts would be "the kiss of death" for Dist. Atty. Ira Reiner, some said. Others attacked Bradley.

Deputy Dist. Atty. Terry White, lead prosecutor in the King beating trial, reacted with "shock first, then disappointment" after the jury returned its 10 not-guilty verdicts.

Photo: James Ruebsamen

In the hours after the King verdicts were announced, a culturally and ethnically diverse crowd gathered to protest outside Parker Center, the downtown police headquarters. Some decried police violence, others the perceived inequities of the criminal justice system. Eventually, the policies of the U.S. government—and the symbol of America—came under attack.

Photo: Todd Bigelow

The early demonstrations in front of Parker Center were relatively peaceful as police faced off against the growing crowd. As night fell, however, the group grew progressively more violent, with some members moving west to City Hall and the Los Angeles Times building, smashing windows along the way. Others set fire to palm trees lining the Hollywood Freeway.

Photo: Rosemary Kaul

They said his statement after the verdicts was tantamount to a license to riot. The news rocked supporters of Police Department reform. They suddenly found themselves facing the possibility that a year's worth of effort had been wiped out in the minutes it took to declare the four officers not guilty. "This will be a big plus for the vote 'no' on the Charter Amendment F campaign," predicted Don Clinton, head of an anti-F group. "It will instill in people the belief that maybe Chief Gates was right all along. Maybe our Police Department is better than we realized."

After learning of the verdicts, Stanley K. Sheinbaum, the president of the city Police Commission, headed for police headquarters. Arriving shortly after 6 p.m., he found his way blocked by a roiling sea of demonstrators. Many were white. There were Progressive Labor Party and Revolutionary Community Party signs. Then someone yanked a man out of the way of Sheinbaum's car. When he drove around back, he caught sight of Gates. The chief was getting in a car.

Where are you going? Sheinbaum asked. Gates answered tersely: He had something to do. As it turned out later, he had chosen that moment to head for the upscale community of Brentwood to attend a fund-raiser for the campaign against Charter Amendment F. It was a decision Gates would come to regret.

Sheinbaum went inside to the police commissioners' office. "They're breaking into the building!" someone shouted. Rocks began flying through windows above the plate-glass doors. Outside, the crowd had swelled to several hundred. Demonstrators were demanding Gates' resignation. A line of police in riot gear inched the crowd back. "There was no justice for Rodney King. Without justice, there will be no peace," warned one protester.

In South Los Angeles, anger had exploded into action. When police officers confronted a crowd at 71st Street and Normandie Avenue, people hurled rocks and bottles. A block away, at Florence Avenue and Normandie, about 200 people milled, many with raised fists. They hurled chunks of pavement at passing cars. Then, people mobbed cars, dragging light-skinned motorists into the street, robbing and beating them.

The worst riots of the century had begun.

Into the storm rumbled Reginald Denny, the truck driver, hauling 27 tons of sand toward an Inglewood cement-mixing plant. At about 6:30 p.m., his 18-wheeler rolled into the intersection. Rocks and bottles whizzed past. Overturned trash cans littered the street. As Denny slowed down, several black men surrounded the rig. One yanked open the truck door and pulled Denny from his cab. At least two others beat him in the head and kicked him, knocking him to the ground. After kicking him, one man raised his hands in triumph. As Denny tried to move, another man bashed his skull with a fire extinguisher from the truck.

The attack was broadcast live on TV.

Watching from his home, T.J. Murphy, a 30-year-old, black, unemployed aerospace engineer, and his friend, Tee Barnett, 28, were appalled. "Somebody's got to get that guy out of there," they said to each other. They headed for the nearby intersection, never thinking the rescue might fall to them. But the police were nowhere to be seen. The injured man—his face awash in blood and his eyes

A half-mile from the corner of Florence and Normandie, you could see the helicopters, swarming. Then, closer in, there were clots of people running, and over the scanner, the sound of police and TV crews telling each other, "Get out of there. Now."

There was gridlock. People lined the sidewalk six deep, shouting, gossiping, shaking their fists. Some held cans of beer and soda, some struggled home with children in their arms. They wore shorts and sport shirts. They looked like they had lined up for a Fourth of July parade.

In traffic, drivers were beginning to panic, pulling out into the paths of oncoming cars to make a quick getaway. As each car approached the intersection, young kids—teen-agers—were loping out, taking a look at the people inside and then heaving chunks of concrete and brick at anyone who wasn't black.

They looked so young, too young for the way their faces contorted with rage. Their wrists seemed so thin, their chests so frail. The rocks would slam into car after car, and you could hear the shouts. "Yeah, m------ f------! Oh, yeah!"

SHAWN HUBLER
Times staff writer

swollen shut—had somehow managed to get back behind the wheel and was making his getaway an inch at a time.

A woman, a nutrition consultant on her way home from work, had hoisted herself onto the side of the truck cab and was shouting steering instructions to Denny. Then she climbed inside to console Denny as a black-clad young man took over the driving. The new driver was unable to see through the shattered windshield, so Murphy clung to the side of the truck and guided him. "You're going to make it," the consultant kept telling Denny, "You're going to be OK."

As the driver tried desperately to speed up the heavy rig, Barnett drove in front of the truck, putting on her hazard lights to try to clear the way. After a trip that seemed to take hours, the rig lurched into the driveway at Daniel Freeman Memorial Hospital. Denny went into a convulsion, spitting up blood. One minute longer, a paramedic said, and the 36-year-old father wouldn't have made it.

In the Crenshaw District, Holly Echols was one of many glued to the television. A 33-year-old media relations manager who is black, she lived with her 9-year-old daughter, Aja. She knew there would be a bad reaction to the verdicts. She had found herself on a three-way call with her sister and her mother. Her mother had cried; none of them could believe the verdicts. "It's going to be worse than '65," Echols' mother predicted. "There's going to be trouble tonight."

By that time, people were honking their horns in protest as they drove up and down Crenshaw Boulevard, just two blocks away. Echols could hear shooting. She turned out the lights. On the television screen, the violence was escalating; people were being yanked from their cars.

"Where are the police? Where the hell are the police? I don't believe this!'" she screamed at the television. "…This is not tape, this is live! And there are no police. There's no ambulance. There's no firemen. What the hell is going on?"

Television anchors, reporters and viewers across the country asked the same question as they watched mobs drag motorists from their cars—beating them to a pulp without any sign of police.

The police, it would turn out, had already come and gone. Earlier, many officers of the 77th Street Division had tried and failed to stop the growing violence. Severely outnumbered, a field commander had ordered his troops to withdraw. They had retreated to a secure, cinder-block-walled bus terminal at 54th Street and Arlington Avenue—an emergency police command center 30 blocks from where Reginald Denny lay.

At about 4:30 p.m., Kris Owen and partner Steve Zaby had heard the first disturbance call: Six black men were smashing car windows with baseball bats. Nearing Florence and 71st, Owen's cruiser was hit by a volley of bricks and rocks. Other officers were attending an injured white driver who had been pulled from his Volvo. Over his portable radio, Owen heard a family had been attacked and beaten in their car near Florence and Normandie. He and Zaby raced to the scene and found a terrified Latino couple with a 1-year-old child. Their faces were bloody, cut by broken glass. Owen and Zaby hustled the family back to the squad car and drove them to the hospital.

An LAPD cruiser is turned over and
set afire on Main Street near City
Hall during the first night of rioting.

Photo: Alan Duignan

As more officers responded, sirens drowned out the noise of the mob. Several patrolmen chased down and hogtied a 16-year-old youth who they said was throwing rocks at the arriving units. The crowd was wild. One irate man pulled down his pants, grabbed his genitals and cursed an officer.

The black officers were singled out for the most vehement abuse. Officer Rashad Sharif, 24, a slender, black police veteran of three years, was kicked, struck, spat on and taunted: "You sellout! You sellout! Why are you working for a white man?" Several in the crowd took up a chilling chant: "It's Uzi time!"

Meanwhile, Lt. Michael Moulin, a ruddy-faced field commander, had arrived at the scene with a contingent of 25 officers from the station. But at 5:43 p.m., he shouted into his radio: "I want everybody out of here. Florence and Normandie. Everybody, get out! Now!" Suddenly, police became scarce. Two officers returned briefly to rescue a Korean woman, unconscious in her car. As one last cruiser passed, full bottles of liquor bounced off its roof, so close to one officer's head he could identify the label: "Kessler."

Back at the station, Detective Lt. Bruce Hagerty took temporary command. Shortly after 6:30 p.m., he saw Reginald Denny getting pummeled over live television. Hagerty ordered the only unit at his command, an undercover car loaded with four plainclothes detectives, to attempt a rescue. Near Florence and Normandie, they were forced to turn back by sniper fire and by streets clogged with rioters and abandoned cars.

So as Holly Echols sat at home, shouting at her television set, the police were idling in a bus terminal, miles from the action. There they sat, sweating under their white helmets and bulletproof vests. All watched Moulin for any hint of gearing up. It would be hours before they were sent out again.

A continent away, the significance of the moment did not elude Gates's designated successor, Philadelphia Police Commissioner Willie L. Williams. The evening, he thought to himself, would prove to be a crucial moment in the history of the department.

As darkness fell, more than 2,000 people gathered at the First A.M.E. Church in the Mid-City area to express their unity against the King verdicts. Rodney King's mother, Angela, appeared briefly before the cheering crowd. In a basement meeting room, surrounded by a small group of clergymen, the church's pastor, the Rev. Cecil L. Murray, closed his eyes and fought back tears. He called the verdicts a tragedy, "not because it's unbelievable, but because it *is* believable."

"If something in you can die," Murray had said that afternoon after watching the verdicts, "that something died."

As gospel music poured forth from the church that night, one television station turned the music into the soundtrack behind its images of mounting chaos— one of the many jarring juxtapositions that Los Angeles seemed to have become.

Once the sun had set, looting and burning began in earnest. One of the first targets was Tom's Liquor and Deli at Florence and Normandie. The first fire call came in at 7:45 p.m. as rampaging rioters began torching buildings in South Los Angeles.

A woman is escorted to safety by an
unidentified man after her car was
pelted with rocks at the intersection
of Normandie and Florence avenues
shortly after the King verdicts were

WEDNESDAY, APRIL 29, 9 P.M.
Manchester and Slauson avenues

A colleague, Mike Meadows, and I were crisscrossing streets, looking for looters, when we drove by a liquor store at Manchester and Slauson. Four guys were taking what they could and were just beginning to start a fire. I was on the sidewalk across from the store when I heard someone behind me yell "M----- F-----, stop taking pictures."

I turned to see a man, standing about 15 foot away, holding a bottle of liquor and aiming a gun at me. He fired. I turned and ran down the street to where Meadows was waiting in the car with the engine running.

The guy fired five or six more shots as I ran.

If he had been sober I don't think I would have made it.

KIRK McKOY
Times photographer

A man fends off would-be looters at a liquor store at 3rd and Berendo streets during the second day of rioting. The man, wearing a white glove, was able to keep the mob at bay until police units arrived at the scene.

Photo: Larry Davis

At 126th Street and Avalon, Nettie Lewis left the View Heights Convalescent Hospital, where she worked, and raced toward home. On Avalon, crowds were gathering. People were shouting, their faces angry. Someone had torched a fast-food chicken restaurant at Imperial Highway. Others were hurling bottles. As Lewis drove through a pandemonium of looting and mayhem, she looked for a side street, wound up on a dead-end, made a furious U-turn and managed to escape. She arrived home crying. Her family was all right, watching the riot unfold on TV.

Basiliso Merino, the Mexican immigrant roofer, had taken his daughter to enroll in Holy Communion classes on West 70th Street that afternoon. Sign up and get out, a church worker said brusquely. It's ugly. Merino didn't understand—until he began driving. Black youths were stoning cars. At home, he could see the first columns of smoke rising on Florence Avenue, just five or six blocks away. His normally quiet side street descended into chaos. Black and Latino neighbors were returning with carloads of looted goods. Children rode stolen bicycles, women carried bags filled with shoes. Some neighbors tried to sell Merino their stolen merchandise. When night fell, Merino's family retreated to the safety of the living

room, watching the fires from behind barred windows. About midnight, a group of men and women arrived to loot the liquor store across the street. One man seemed to be pouring gasoline.

"My God, this is it," Merino thought. "They're going to burn down the whole neighborhood!"

For the Los Angeles Fire Department, the night brought tremors of terror, acts of courage, moments of tenderness and irony. Their usual enemy, fire, was overwhelming. Worse, they served as targets for rioters using firearms, bottles and rocks against any convenient symbol of authority. The police, their command in apparent disarray, provided little protection. It all happened so fast. Conflagrations that normally drew 10 companies were handled by one. Hostile crowds taunted firefighters. Gunfire rattled in the night.

Capt. Paul Butler's hook-and-ladder company found a fire at a department store at Vermont and Vernon. They set up lines to keep the blaze from endangering looters in a nearby market. Suddenly, four armed men confronted the firefighters. Two AK-47s, a shotgun and a pistol were trained on Butler's crew. The leader stuck a gun in Butler's face.

An unidentified Asian man was in the wrong place at the wrong time. Two hours after the Rodney King verdicts were announced, he walked to a bus stop at Florence and Normandie avenues where he was severely beaten and robbed. He was later led to safety by an unidentified man.

Photos: Kirk McKoy

A tear gave witness to the reaction of the Rev. Cecil L. Murray, pastor of the 8,000-member First A.M.E. Church, as the verdicts were announced. "You think rational people will be at least semi-rational. ... But to come back and see them completely whitewashing something that the whole world witnessed—this is a brutalization of truth."

Photo: Robert Gabriel

Butler banished a fleeting notion of trying to disarm the gunman. As a hostile crowd gathered, Butler thought that if he would give the man something—a trophy for his troubles—maybe he would go away. Butler offered the man his radios—$3,000 hunks of electronic hardware. Then, still at gunpoint, he and three of his firemen ran for safety, leaving the fire and their trucks behind.

"As we were running away from the rigs, the people were sitting around, cheering these guys on. 'Kill 'em! Shoot 'em!' " Apparatus Operator Dennis Waite recalled.

Not far away, firefighter Tom Carroll spotted a car coming up fast on the right. He was perched at the rear of a hook-and-ladder as it raced, siren wailing, through the flaming chaos of Western Avenue. Up ahead, looters and spectators ran wildly in an intersection. The driver, Scott Miller, slowed down to figure out how to get through. Capt. Francis Howard sat at his side; firefighter Paul Jordan behind. Suddenly the car, its headlights off, darted past. What was this guy doing?

"A gun reached out," Carroll recalled later, "and there was a flash."

There was a second of silence, maybe two, then Jordan's voice crackling over the radio headset: "Scott's been hit! Scott's been hit!"

Howard saw Miller sagging toward the steering wheel, chin resting on chest. Blood gushed from his cheek. Jordan yelled for help. Carroll ran to Miller's aid. The ladder truck would have to serve as an ambulance. Cedars-Sinai Medical Center, they decided, offered the best hope of saving Miller. Jordan maneuvered the truck northward, dodging cars and people, racing past flaming stores and frenzied looters. He slowed at intersections but barreled through, trusting that the motorists would heed the siren. Howard later would call it, "Mr. Toad's Wild Ride."

Miller was conscious but very weak. A call had been put ahead to the hospital. A gurney would have to be waiting outside because the firetruck was too large for the driveway that leads to the subterranean emergency room. Miller was lowered to the gurney and rushed inside. The 32-year-old father of two underwent 5 1/2 hours of emergency surgery to remove the bullet. It had slammed into his right cheek, slashed his interior carotid artery and lodged in his neck. The blood loss caused a stroke that had paralyzed his left arm.

Throughout South Los Angeles, poor Latino residents joined their black neighbors in looting the hundreds of liquor stores and discount clothing outlets that lined Florence, Figueroa, Slauson and other thoroughfares. At the corner of Slauson and Vermont, hundreds of people ransacked the Indoor Swap Meet. Pregnant women emerged carrying boxes of diapers and baby food. It was clear: The protest over police abuse had become a poverty riot. Latino residents who had barely heard of Rodney King helped bend back iron security bars so they could loot at will.

Myung Lee had fled her doughnut shop early. "Get out!" the voice on the telephone had said. It was another Korean merchant several blocks east, at Florence and Normandie. William Hong had fled his liquor store, too. In the confusing overlay of TV pictures—the cameras shifted from South Los Angeles to

WEDNESDAY, APRIL 29, 3:45 P.M.
First A.M.E. Church, Mid-City

The mood at the First A.M.E. Church was somber. One could still see the shock and disbelief on the faces of the church members and all who gathered to watch as the verdicts were read.

"Not guilty, not guilty, not guilty. "

Then I saw the Rev. Cecil (Chip) Murray.

Pounding his fist into his left hand, he began to cry.

"They gave us nothing, nothing. Not even a bone, dear God, not even a bone."

I have seen men cry at the joy of birth and the loss of death. I have seen men cry for the dream of peace. Now, joy and peace seem far away.

KIRK McKOY
Times photographer

At the corner of Florence and Normandie avenues, mob rule filled the vacuum left by the retreat of the LAPD. Overwhelmed by the size and ire of the crowd, police pulled back, though some officers made daring solo runs into the area to save beleaguered motorists.

Photo: Kirk McKoy

police headquarters to Compton, tracking an ever-widening circle of fiery destruction—Lee at home in North Hollywood and Hong at home in Simi Valley found it impossible to tell whether their stores had survived.

Leticia, the unemployed illegal immigrant from Mexico City, had been caught in traffic during the first outburst of rioting and had rushed to her apartment, next to Hong's liquor store. She called her roommate, Anna, at work. Get back here! she insisted. By the time Anna made it home, people were looting Hong's store. They were breaking the windows in the doughnut shop, busting into the video store where Leticia had rented a tape hours before. Most of the women in the apartment building joined in. Why not? they figured. Everyone else was doing it. Leticia went inside Hong's store. It was muddy and slippery. Everybody was pushing and shoving. Many of the apartment residents took milk, butter and other food. Leticia, who has no children, did not.

"We told ourselves we were taking things because we were needy. Because we were poor. But when we got home and saw what we had taken, there was only beer," she said. She drank so much "free" beer she got drunk and went to sleep.

Anna locked herself inside the apartment until a neighbor came to warn them that a group of black men—led by a neighbor they knew only as Mike—was about to torch Hong's liquor store and the other Asian-owned storefronts. They held crude torches made of sticks. "They were thinking of every excuse they could to burn the building," Anna said later. " 'This Korean cheated us.' 'This other Korean was mean to us.' " Anna pleaded with them not to burn the building: "Go somewhere else. You'll burn my house down. There's families with children living next door." Mike knew Anna; she was cool. He agreed not to torch Hong's store. The mob set fire to a grocery across the street instead.

Marcus and Cletus, meanwhile, had joined the looting in Cletus' neighborhood. But they didn't feel satisfied; the act of taking was not an act of retribution. Something had to be destroyed. If only we had a car, they thought. We could hit Westwood, somewhere like that. As it was, they walked to a store on 67th Street and West Boulevard in the Hyde Park District near Inglewood. They found four Latino friends. Marcus kicked in the door of the store. They loaded themselves down with what they could carry—canned goods, beer and food—and headed back to their neighborhood.

But once home, Cletus and Marcus started worrying. Had they left fingerprints? Had they been caught on tape by a security camera? They had to go back. From a shelf, Cletus pulled down oil that he kept for kerosene lamps. They poured it into a 40-ounce beer bottle and used a rag for a wick. When they got to the store, looters were still cleaning it out. The men yelled a warning, waited until the store was empty and threw the bottle against the wall. Poof! The bottle exploded into fire. That *felt* like something.

By 9 p.m., normal life throughout Los Angeles had been derailed. Every police officer in the city had been ordered to report for duty. Public and parochial schools were being shut down in a 30-square-mile area. Children were to stay at home, indoors. Dozens of bus lines in South Los Angeles were being halted. With the rioting spreading to Inglewood, Mayor Bradley declared a local state of emergency. Minutes later, at Bradley's request, Gov. Wilson ordered the National Guard to activate 2,000 reserve soldiers.

The demonstration at police headquarters had turned violent. Protesters set fire to a kiosk, so the police line moved to break up the crowd. People turned and ran, fanning out through the area, vandalizing other buildings, smashing cars and hurtling newspaper boxes through plate-glass windows. They stopped off at City Hall, then the Los Angeles Times building, where they broke out nearly every first-floor window, pelted third-floor newsroom windows with concrete chunks and trashed some first-floor offices. Others headed for the Hollywood Freeway, torching palm trees. As rioters lunged out into the freeway traffic, a few panicked drivers turned and fled against oncoming cars.

At 9:05 p.m., the California Highway Patrol closed many freeway exit ramps on the Harbor Freeway in hopes of keeping unsuspecting motorists from wandering into the path of violence. At Los Angeles International Airport, the Federal Aviation Administration shifted the landing pattern of approaching jetliners after the police reported that one of their helicopters had been fired upon. Suddenly, it seemed, everyone had guns. Dozens of pawnshops and other businesses stocked with firearms were systematically looted during the first few hours of the unrest, putting thousands of guns onto the streets. On South Western Avenue, suspected gang members broke into the Western Surplus store and carted off as many as 1,700 guns, plus ammunition. Outside the riot-damaged areas, fearful residents crowded into gun stores, clamoring for firearms. They bought the only ones immediately available—surplus rifles from World War II.

By late Wednesday, authorities would report that at least 10 people had been killed, nine of them shooting victims. Nearly two dozen injured people, including five gunshot victims, had been admitted to the emergency room at Martin Luther King Jr./Drew Medical Center. Over the next few days, the vast majority of shooting victims would be killed not by police officers or soldiers, as in the Watts riots, but by gun-toting rioters. Burning and beatings would produce the most indelible images during the riots, but bullets would account for the greatest human wreckage.

The deadliest part of Los Angeles Wednesday night was the heart of Watts. Far from the television cameras, as blazes roared through shops on the perimeter of the Nickerson Gardens housing project, police fired 88 rounds in firefights with snipers. "It was anarchy, total anarchy," said Lt. Michael Hillman of the LAPD's Metro Division. "You had people running in the streets, looting, shooting at firefighters, shooting at police. Total chaos."

Nearby, Dennis (Bull) Jackson and Anthony (Romeo) Taylor were doing what they usually did on warm spring nights, according to friends—hanging out in the parking lot near Jackson's apartment, drinking beer. This time, friends said, the pair got their liquor for free. Shortly after 11 p.m., nearby gunfire caused a dozen or more men in the parking lot to scatter. When the shots stopped, Jackson and Taylor were dead. A friend said officers across the streets had fired on the parking lot because a man, wearing a hood and waving a handgun, had bounded through the area firing at other officers down the block.

WEDNESDAY, APRIL 29, 8 P.M.
The Civic Center

You could hear them from four blocks away, roaring like drunken fans at a Raiders game. Then, suddenly, they were on the move. The crowd of rioters, turned away moments earlier by helmeted Los Angeles police officers in front of Parker Center, streamed west, down 1st Street.

Along the way, the mob vented its rage on inanimate objects—car hoods and windshields, mailboxes, newspaper boxes, shuttered doors and windows.

One man dressed in a khaki military cap and fatigues launched a series of karate kicks on a mailbox. With each ferocious kick, he twisted and dented the metal a little more.

Then he looked up and saw a group of Times employees watching from a second floor balcony. The rioter grinned and waved. "Hey, man, come on down and join us! Join the fun!" He ran off, laughing.

STEPHEN BRAUN
Times staff writer

Feelings run high at 36th Street
and Vermont Avenue in South Los
Angeles during the civil unrest as
Harold Jones talks to LAPD Sgt.
Jim Nolan.

Photo: Patrick Downs

Although Jackson and Taylor were shot around 11:10 p.m., officers pinned down by gunfire were unable to recover their bodies and pronounce them dead until 12:15 a.m. They used a six-ton armored personnel carrier to re-enter the area. Jackson, according to a preliminary coroner's account, was shot in the back, and his body was found inside his front door. A bullet passed through Taylor's head and neck, the coroner said, and his body was found outside the building. No weapons were recovered. Officers said they did not know whether Taylor had been shooting. But they believed Jackson, based on his clothing, was the gunman firing from the corner of the building.

By Wednesday evening, word of the anarchy in Los Angeles had reached the King jurors at home with their families in Ventura County. Images of fire, looting and shooting flickered on their television sets. Pundits were second-guessing their deliberations, speculating about pro-police bias and racism. In the days following, some jurors would have their phones disconnected. Others would leave town or seek police protection.

"This is the worst experience of my life," one juror confessed. "I don't know what's in the hearts of the others, but I know in my heart I'm not a racist.... Personally, it's been a little hell. I can't believe all of this is a reaction to what we did."

In the hours after the verdicts, the jurors began to unburden themselves, privately. One said the verdicts had not been even a close call. They had been swayed not by the videotape, but by what transpired before the camera started rolling: King had refused to leave his car; he seemed dangerous to them, menacing. If he had complied with orders from the police as they tried to arrest him, the jurors believed, the beating never would have occurred.

One juror said the group found the officers' testimony credible. They did not believe race was a factor in the beating. They felt the officers acted within the scope of LAPD guidelines. Police work is tough, explained one juror. "They're policemen, they're not angels," she said. "They're out there to do a low-down dirty job. Would you want your husband doing it, or your son or your father?"

As for Rodney King himself, he retreated to the solitude of his bedroom, shaking and speechless. He had watched the verdicts on television. Stunned, he had reached for a pack of Marlboro Lights. "He wasn't talking in clear sentences," said one friend. "It suddenly was like he had no idea who he was or what time it was or where he was. He would start to make sense, and then 10 seconds later he couldn't even tell you what room he was in. Then he went in the bedroom." King locked himself in. The lights were off, the television turned down low. On the screen, the officers who had beaten King were hugging and smiling, free men. Through the door, King's occasional screams could be heard. "Why? Why? Why?" he groaned. "Why are they beating me again?"

WEDNESDAY, APRIL 29, 6:30 P.M.
A restaurant at Pico Boulevard and Fairfax Avenue

The first radio reports of the violence were coming in as I drove to a long-planned dinner date at Walia, an Ethiopian restaurant in a block of Indian shops. There was only one other party of diners. The woman running the place was warm and attentive, but every time she left our table she rushed back to sit tensely in the corner near a small black-and-white television, watching live coverage of the city unhinging.

"It's horrible," she told us once when she came to check on our drinks. "They are pulling people out of cars and beating them."

Half oblivious, I'm now embarrassed to say, my friend and I ate, drank and talked. As we were about to leave we were startled as the other group of diners jumped up and ran out. While we paid our bill, the woman told us that rocks had been thrown at cars on Pico. She nervously unlocked the door and we hurried out. As I drove away I could feel my complacency breaking down.

The next day, Walia and the Indian shops went up in flames as the woman watched from across the street. The entire scene was on live television.

JOYCE MILLER
Los Angeles Times Magazine

Art Washington, who owns a pest control business, shakes his fist at looters while holding a hammer with the other hand. In defending his shop on Western Avenue, Washington became one of the scores of Los Angeles business operators who took up arms to protect their property during the unrest.

AWAKENING TO A NIGHTMARE

5

THURSDAY, APRIL 30, 1992

The second day of rioting arrived in a blazing rage. Between midnight and 3 a.m., three reports of fire were coming in every minute. Mayor Bradley imposed a citywide, dusk-to-dawn curfew: Public places would be off-limits, ammunition sales prohibited and gasoline sales banned except for normal filling up. Two thousand National Guard troops were heading for Los Angeles. At a midnight press conference, Gov. Wilson warned grimly, "We are determined that this city is not going to suffer the kind of terrorizing that some people seem bent on inflicting upon it."

Los Angeles, nevertheless, awoke to a living nightmare.

William Hong couldn't sleep. He left his Simi Valley home at 4 a.m. to reach his South-Central liquor store before dawn. From the freeway, he could see fires glowing across South Los Angeles. At Florence and Figueroa, several businesses had been razed. Kitty-cornered from his own business, a black-owned grocery store had been burned to the ground. At his store, the windows had been smashed, iron security bars ripped out, but nothing had been charred.

Art Washington, too, made a nervous 4 a.m. drive to his pest control business at Western Avenue and 20th Street, a place he had assumed was far enough north of the hot spots to be safe. The 53-year-old black businessman telephoned his wife, Georgia: "They got in." The computers were gone. The windows were broken. Most of the office furniture remained. There were no fires.

After daybreak, though, it started again. The athletic shoe store next door became a magnet for young looters. Across 20th Street, dozens of spectators lounged at a 24-hour taco stand. There were no police. Any minute, Washington thought, they're going to try to burn down this side of the block. Finally, a dozen police officers—having fought a guerrilla war with looters a block north at Western and Washington—made their way to Washington's mini-mall and pushed the looters back to the other side of the street. From the taco stand, looters threw rocks and shards of glass. Washington stood in front of his business, watching.

Then he lost control. He grabbed a hammer and walked across the street into the faces of the looters, screaming at them hysterically. "I worked for that!" he shouted. "Not *you*! Don't burn down none of my business! I worked too *hard* for this!...It's not right what y'all do! I came from the ghetto, too, like you! You call this black power?"

Nobody in the crowd responded. They looked at Washington as if he were crazy. Near the corner of Florence and Normandie, a 21-year-old man named Eugene was defiant. He acknowledged taking a few beers from the liquor store, even trying to break into the gas station safe. Rocks were flying across the street. Eugene wasn't afraid—not even after invading rival gang turf. Crips and Bloods had joined ranks.

THURSDAY, APRIL 30, 4 P.M.
Mid-Town Shopping Center

The shops were filled with smoke and fire, looters were coming in droves. Maybe they heard it on radio or TV, or by word of mouth, but they knew that a market—in this case, The Boys—had just been split open and was full of food, liquor, radios and cigarettes.

There was a crush of people trying to get in, and some cars already full of loot trying to get out.

As fire nearby raged out of control, several police cars and hook and ladder trucks careened by, not stopping. One woman zoomed up to the front of the building in a late model Seville, a wild look in her eyes and a grin on her face. She jumped out of her car without rolling up the windows, leaving her screaming infant unattended. Then, the well-dressed, professional-looking woman sprinted into the store for her share. Inside the market, there was pandemonium.

As I scribbled notes furiously, one looter, dragging what appeared to be a small copying machine, tapped me on the shoulder and said calmly, "I know you're a reporter, but can you help me drag this outside?" I said no. He went on dragging.

JOSH MEYER
Times staff writer

"Ain't no reason to be afraid," he scoffed. "Everybody's together. I see Hoovers and 8 Trey Gangsters, even Bloods....There ain't anybody scared of nothin' out here."

As police approached, Eugene stood his ground. "We ain't afraid of them," he boasted. "We got guns just like them." When the police stopped, they met outright hostility. "Go on, harass me!" one young black man shouted, taunting a group of officers. Several more police cars screeched to the intersection and the young man and his friends suddenly were gone. "Where you running?" one officer jeered.

The violence was no longer confined to one area. Along every major thoroughfare running from Koreatown into South-Central Los Angeles, businesses were being sacked. With thick smoke clouding the air and car horns and burglar alarms blaring, looters swarmed dozens of stores Thursday with seemingly little fear of reprisal. Looter gridlock snarled parking lots and streets. Carting off everything from guns to diapers, some people expressed fury over the King verdicts, but others went about their work in high spirits, seeming to enjoy the anarchy.

Octavio Sandoval, a 17-year-old high school junior, paid a visit to the Hi Brite Furniture Store on Vermont Avenue. It looked like fun, so he and two friends walked out with three beds. Cars stopped for them as they crossed the street. Back home, Sandoval gave bunk beds to his younger brother and sister. He kept another bed for himself, so he would no longer have to sleep on the floor. "I felt I was doing something good for my family," he said later.

As Sandoval saw it, he wasn't hurting anybody's business: The furniture people had insurance. He didn't feel like he was stealing, because the police didn't say anything. "By not stopping us, they allowed us to break the law," he said. Nor did he mind that Latinos, his own people, were doing a lot of the looting. "We're accustomed to being a low minority here," he said. "So I thought, 'Let us have fun while we can.'" But his mother disapproved of the stealing, and Sandoval feared the police would come. So two days later, he took the beds to a nearby Catholic church where officials had encouraged looters to surrender stolen goods.

Like a bandage stripped off an open wound, the unrest seemed to lay bare the racial anger long simmering among the city's ethnic communities. The popular notion that Los Angeles was transforming itself into a harmonious, multiethnic model city seemed to waft away in the smoke billowing over the city. Each new televised image—black, Latino and white looters rampaging through ruined stores, mostly white police officers and National Guard soldiers, dazed motorists beaten by angry black assailants, frightened Korean merchants guarding their shuttered markets with guns—threatened to reinforce fears and prejudices.

Across South Los Angeles, blacks, whites, Latinos and Asians met in violent confrontations. Inside homes and offices, people reacted with anger and suspicion. A white Simi Valley doctor said the riots gave credence to the officers' defense that their lives are threatened every day: "Yesterday, I would have found them guilty. Today, I probably wouldn't." Said a 42-year-old African-American who

Scene at sunrise the day after the
King verdicts at a shopping mall at
the corner of 17th Street and
Western Avenue: Looters loaded
booty into their vehicles. During the
day, the crush of looters trying to
get into and out of store parking
lots would create gridlock in many
areas of the city.

Photo: Rick Meyer

As dusk descended on Los Angeles the day after the riots began, fires continued to light up the evening sky. And for the second night in a row, firefighters were outgunned by the forces on the streets. In some locations, such as this mini-mall at 6th Street and Western Avenue, citizens armed only with garden hoses tried in vain to help out.

Photo: Jim Mendenhall

Traffic was near gridlock. Signals were out. A thick funnel of smoke rose from an attic shared by six storefronts, while next door, looters were piling office furniture into the back of a pickup truck. Bedlam reigned.

I stopped the car. The photographer with me began shooting pictures of the firefighters in action.

Vermont looked as if it had been bombed. The entire east side of the block was filled with the blackened rubble of shops, their windows and facades missing.

As we walked, we encountered a shirtless black man and his son, about 7, viewing the rubble. The man, who declined to give his name, talked of having heard all about Watts when he was young. Now, he wanted to show his own son the horrors of lawlessness. "It's stupid," he said bitterly. "It's just stupid."

DAVID FERRELL
Times staff writer

owned a business in the Slauson area: "Blacks did it to themselves this time. They shot themselves in the foot."

Tensions between the black and Korean communities had been high for some time, inflamed by the Latasha Harlins killing. Now many of the burned and looted stores belonged to Korean-American merchants. Some rioters said they were avenging the girl's death. But if the goal was to punish Koreans, the vengeance got out of control. The victims included people of all ethnic groups—residents of economically depressed neighborhoods that, once again, were unraveling.

Sitting forlornly in his plundered car audio store in South Los Angeles, Eddie Rho, 36, surmised that the looters had been black. The store was targeted, he said, because of the expensive stereo equipment he sold. But he also wondered if it was because he is Korean.

"From now on I can try to be close to them," he said, "but they won't be close to us."

Across the city, people puzzled over who was pillaging their communities. The answer seemed to be both criminals and opportunists. All races took part. There were gang members and mothers with children. "You had 7- and 8-year-olds all the way up to 60-year-olds," said a woman named Dorothy who watched the rioting in the Crenshaw area. "You had everyday citizens.... I thought about participating myself."

Onlookers raced to stricken neighborhoods to watch, join in the looting or videotape the mayhem. Gleeful teen-agers and families, as if on a weekend outing, ignored outnumbered police and loaded up. Jim Galipeau, a veteran deputy probation officer in his department's gang unit, said there was a strong gang presence. But he discounted the notion that the activity was organized. "This is just people who are greedy and immoral and opportunistic," he said. "They don't give a [expletive] about Rodney King."

At intersection after intersection, cars crept along jammed streets in stricken areas and motorists leaned out of windows flashing "black power" signs. Many honked their horns and chanted slogans vilifying the police. A driver who had looted a furniture store drove along with a mattress and a five-piece dinette set lashed to the roof of the car. "I'm really not like this," said Karen, a 24-year-old mother who sat in her car at a mini-mall as her daughter and two nieces filled the back seat with stolen videos and beauty supplies.

By 8 a.m., the National Guard troops had reached armories in the Los Angeles area. For the next several hours, they would pass time taking refresher courses and waiting for equipment, ammunition and deployment orders. In Washington, President Bush denounced the riots as "purely criminal" and offered federal aid to help repair riot damage. At an early-morning news conference, Chief Gates admitted that the Police Department had been "simply overwhelmed." Later, he conceded that it took much longer than he had expected to control the unrest. "My timetable was to contain it last night," he said. "If not last night, today at noon....[Now] hopefully it will be this evening."

Where had the police been? It was a question many were asking.

With thick smoke clouding the air and car horns and burglar alarms blaring, crowds of looters swarmed stores with seemingly little fear of reprisal. They pilfered merchandise from mini malls and swap moots throughout a combat zone that stretched from near downtown into South Los Angeles, through the heart of Hollywood and toward the Westside. While this couple dragged their goods across Vermont Avenue at 2nd Street in Koreatown, a mini-mall went up in flames nearby.

Photo: Jim Mendenhall

THURSDAY, APRIL 30, 11 P.M.
Crenshaw Boulevard near Slauson Avenue

Something remained orderly even during the riot. Someone had ripped the front end of a Versateller in the Crenshaw Town Center. A crowd of men, women and children gathered and formed a line and began helping themselves to the money. One person would grab a handful of money and move out of the way for the next person.

The CHP showed up within minutes, garbed in riot gear and carrying pump-action shotguns. The crowd quickly melted away. The CHP officers had a look of disbelief. They said they didn't know how long they would continue to guard the money.

LEE HARRIS
Times staff writer

The department, it became apparent Thursday, had failed to mobilize fully before the verdicts. When the verdicts came down, most of the force's 1,000 detectives had gone home. Nevertheless, at 6:30 p.m. Wednesday, just as Reginald Denny's gravel truck was rumbling toward Florence and Normandie, Gates said his officers were handling the situation "calmly, maturely, professionally," and he headed for the anti-police-reform fund-raiser in Brentwood. When it was clear that the department lacked the manpower to put down the unrest, there were no attempts to keep unsuspecting motorists out of harm's way.

"It is absolutely inexcusable for the Police Department not to have cordoned off major streets and rerouted traffic," said Detective Zvonko G. (Bill) Pavelic. "They took no action to defuse the situation and stop citizens from becoming victims."

Others accused Gates of purposely delaying the deployment of officers, though there was no evidence of that. "It's his revenge against the people who are trying to put him out of office," said Craig Freis, a candidate for the Los Angeles County Board of Supervisors.

But two of Gates' harshest critics on the Police Commission, President Stanley K. Sheinbaum and Vice President Jesse Brewer, said the chief handled the situation as well as possible. The rioting exposed how thin the 7,900-officer LAPD had become, Sheinbaum said. Gates, he said, "doesn't have the resources to do what needs to be done." Nonetheless, he said the initial deployment of officers would be investigated, particularly the "critical question" of why police apparently did not respond to the first televised scenes of violence.

Meanwhile, citizens were taking security into their own hands.

With a handful of employees, 45-year-old Richard Breen had spent Wednesday night guarding the six-acre, fenced compound that housed his $40-million South-Central trucking company. When dawn came, he figured he had escaped disaster. But later Thursday, the phone rang at his Hollywood Hills home. "We have to evacuate," a worker said. "There're 300 people on the streets rioting." Breen sped back and found rioters gathered in front of the main entrance. After sneaking in through the back, he discovered that his employees were trapped. Hundreds of looters were running past the building from several nearby stores that had been set ablaze. "Their eyes are empty because they have no hope," Breen thought of the looters. "People with empty eyes will do anything."

He armed his employees with handguns and prepared for the worst.

Someone rammed a car into a paper company across the street. The car was in flames. Fearing that a fire at the paper company could wipe out the entire block, Breen called the Fire Department. "They told me, 'You're on your own. There's nothing we can do to help you.' The fires were going 360 degrees around my building." Eventually, the car fire died. Breen settled in for another sleepless night, on guard.

From tiny liquor stores in South-Central to the upscale boutiques in Mid-Wilshire, Korean store owners turned their pastel-colored mini-malls into fortresses. For many, the riots had become a watershed in the struggle for community survival. They had become vigilantes, embracing a brutal new code of order, inflaming whatever fragile relationship they had forged with their black and Latino customers.

From the rooftop of Richard Rhee's supermarket at the corner of 5th and Western, a group of Koreans armed with shotguns and automatic weapons peered out on the smoky streets. Scores of others, carrying steel pipes, pistols and automatic rifles, paced through the parking lot. "It's just like war," said Rhee, a survivor of the Korean War, the Watts riots and three decades of business in Los Angeles. "I'll shoot and worry about the law later."

Korean-language radio stations put out a call for volunteer security guards. Koreans from all over rushed to Koreatown, spearheaded by a small group of elite Korean marine veterans. Even with guns, they seemed at times overwhelmed. For hours Thursday, employees at a mini-mall at Santa Monica and Vermont fought a back-and-forth battle with several hundred looters who surged into the parking lot, retreated when the police arrived and returned shortly after the police left.

In the San Fernando Valley, John Silva, a 44-year-old Vietnam veteran and father of four, hired two security guards to protect his Pacoima meat market. He took to welding the doors shut at night and welding them open in the morning. He stationed his own employees on the roof with a pistol and a shotgun. Then he gave them the following instructions: If you see five or six people coming into the store at night, they are trespassing. So go ahead and holler at them. If there are more than 10 or 15 and they ignore you, show them your weapon. "Now, if that doesn't work, shoot up in the air one time. Now, if that doesn't work, they're trespassing."

Jittery Southern Californians flocked to buy guns Thursday—only to be turned away, in many cases because of a state law prohibiting the same-day sale of contemporary rifles and shotguns. In Anaheim, where there was no ban on ammunition sales, lines formed at about noon. As many as 3,000 customers crowded into Beach Cities Armoury in Hermosa Beach. The shop's complete inventory of antique rifles and pistols was snapped up early in the day. "People were upset about the [state's 15-day] waiting period," said the manager, Steve Mitchell. "They would ask, 'What am I going to do to protect my family if they come over here?'"

Big Ed, the 40-year-old white owner of a machine shop in Long Beach, took to carrying a 9-millimeter weapon around the shop. It made him furious, living and working in an area where there was looting and violence. "Because Rodney King got the s--- kicked out of him doesn't mean that you can go downtown, grab a guy out of his car and damn near kill him," he said. "It's ludicrous! It's anarchy! It's bull!"

If people had jobs and houses and were working hard to support a family, Ed thought, they wouldn't be tearing things up. "What we want is a good honest living," he said. "And what we are finding out is, we're not going to get it. You think the blacks are going to riot? Someday the whites will. And when that happens, that's when your country's going to go.... I know people who are armed to the teeth.

THURSDAY, APRIL 30, 12:15 P.M.
Vermont Avenue, near Downtown

It went from chaotic to ridiculous. Looters created a human wave as they dove over a fence seeking cover when a Korean man with a gun leaned out of the passenger side of a red van and fired two shots in the air—Boom! Boom!

In response, the looters, who outnumbered police, began chanting, "Get them! Kill the bastards!" They didn't. An hour later, I saw a small Suzuki Samurai with a huge couch strapped on the back pass by—to cheers.

DAVID REYES
Times staff writer

Tony Meeks, left, loads a pistol as he helps Norman Simples guard his store at Vermont and Manchester avenues. The two were awaiting protection of the National Guard, which by then was deploying troops throughout the riot-ravaged area.

Photo: Lacy Atkins

Armed Koreans defended their
property as gunfights broke out in
Koreatown at Western Avenue and
5th Street. Hundreds of Korean
businesses were damaged or
destroyed during the unrest.

Photo: Hyungwon Kang

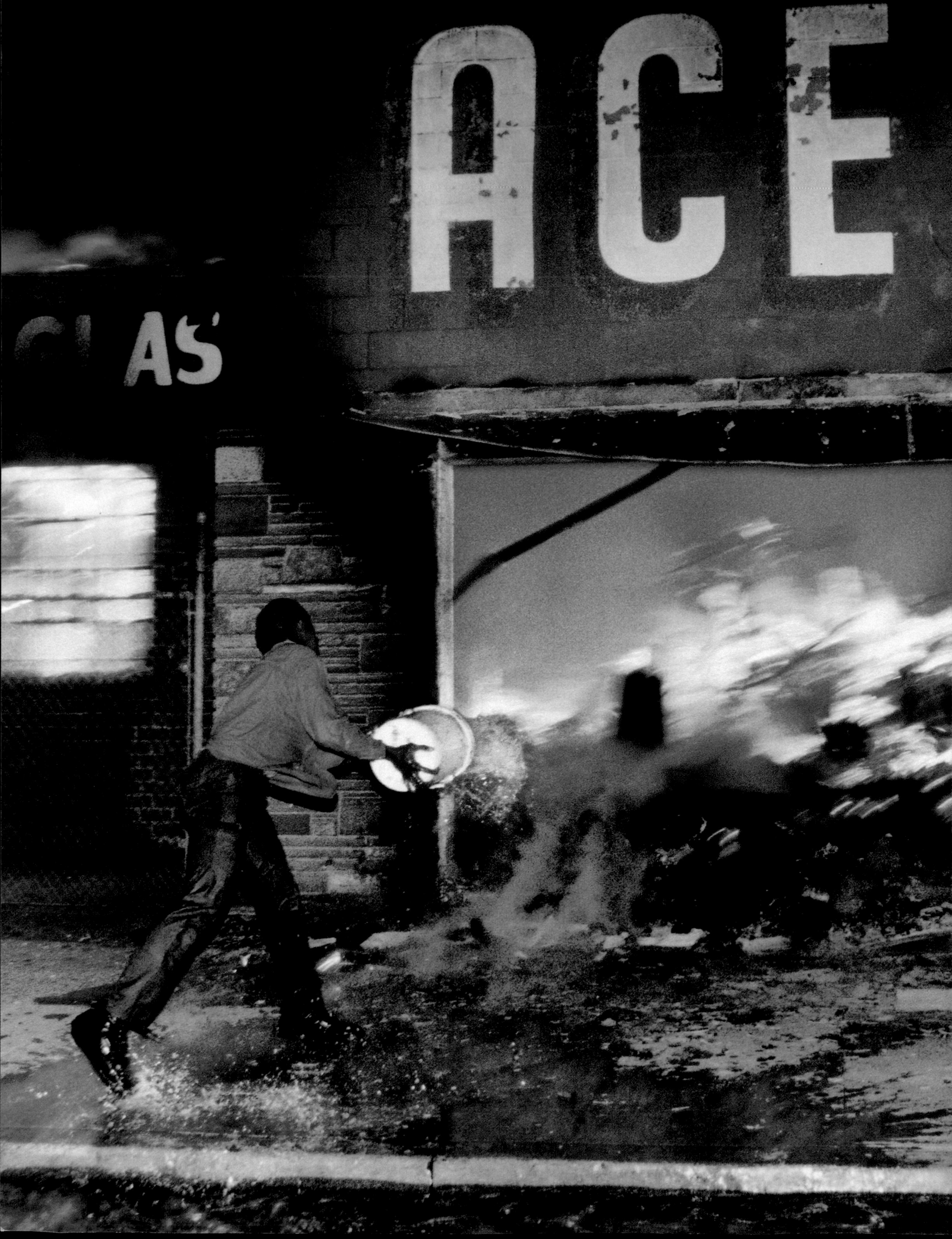
ACE
GLAS

As the Ace Glass shop at Western and Slauson avenues was engulfed in flames, Cornelius Pettus, 33, owner of a nearby market, bravely—but futilely—fought the blaze with a bucket and some water.

Photo: Hyungwon Kang

Koreatown residents helped firefighters by stretching a hose across Western Avenue near 6th Street, where an apartment house was set ablaze. About 850 families were left homeless by the unrest.

Photo: Mike Meadows

They are sick and tired of it and they're not going to put up with it."

At midday, about 200 blacks and Latinos smashed through the gates of the Watts Labor Community Action Committee, an anti-poverty organization that had brought jobs and social services to Watts after the 1965 riots. Inside, armed staff members held off the rioters—for maybe five minutes. Then looters chased them down Central Avenue, shooting, and set the complex on fire.

Sixteen vehicles used to ferry Watts residents to shopping centers and medical offices were burned or vandalized. The offices were reduced to a pile of charcoal between roofless walls. Also destroyed were the contents of the commercial center—including a coin laundry, toy store, youth enterprise project, furniture and appliance shop, and food stamp office. Earnings from the commercial center helped pay for a homeless shelter, job training center and a senior citizens' housing project.

Daily life in parts of South Los Angeles had been grueling enough before the rioting. In some sections, the nearest full-service grocery stores were at least two bus rides away. Neighborhood mom-and-pop stores sometimes charged as much as 30% more than bigger retailers. Fewer than 35 major supermarkets and 20 banks and thrifts served a 35-square-mile area of more than half a million people. Residents routinely stood in lines for hours to make a deposit or cash a check. In some areas, armored trucks would roll to job sites on paydays to cash checks for workers.

Looting and arson were setting back years of efforts to rebuild the community. In recent months, there had been signs that those efforts were paying off. Developments were planned. Large banks seemed to be yielding to pressure to commit more money for small business and home loans.

Now came fears that investment would once again dry up. One of the biggest problems would be insurance, already costly and difficult to obtain. "To the extent you can get insurance now, you're paying a minimum of 25% to 30% more in South Los Angeles," said Greg Boyd of the Economic Resources Corp., a South Los Angeles economic development company. "Now, you may not get insurance at all."

In a smoky parking lot, Ruby Galude, 55, stared in disbelief at the wreckage of her local grocery store. "I'm a diabetic. This is where I get all my juices and foods. What am I going to do now?" A few miles away, Paul C. Hudson arrived at his family-run Broadway Federal Savings & Loan, a community fixture since 1947. Only the exterior wall still stood. There were some brave pronouncements of commitment to the future, but there were also angry accusations that years of economic injustice and neglect set the stage for violence.

Property seemed to have special symbolism to the vandals. While residents raised their fists at police cars and cried, "No justice! No peace!" it was retailers, industrial sites and other enterprises that received the brunt of the rage. Some community leaders sought to offer insight into the violence. The outburst, said Carl Dickerson, president of the Black Business Assn. of Los Angeles, came in part because many people associated the King verdicts with "economic injustice" in their own lives. "They should have jobs and opportunities, but they don't," Dickerson said. "The recession has resulted in a reduction of jobs, mergers have

THURSDAY, APRIL 30, 6:30 P.M.
3rd and Catalina streets, Koreatown

The Jon's supermarket is filling with smoke, water is cascading through the ceiling as firefighters try to extinguish a blaze in the store next door. The entire block seems about to go up. None of this has stopped 200 men, women and children from looting the store.

A 10-year-old boy runs out with a shopping bag. "Whatcha got?" I ask. The boy breaks into a nervous smile. The bag is full of candy and bubble gum, just like Halloween.

Half a dozen LAPD officers watch the spectacle from a block away. They are here only to protect the firefighters. Aren't they going to stop the looting? One of the officers shrugs his shoulders. It's useless, he says. "We chase them out and they run back in."

HECTOR TOBAR
Times staff writer

Two elderly men went into Security Pacific National Bank. They came out quickly. "Isn't the bank open?" one of them asked. They were informed that the bank had been opened by looters smashing the front door. The people inside were not bank employees.

Earlier, several clean-cut young men arrived in a BMW. One went into the bank with a tire iron and smashed the camera. Then he joined the looters stealing computers and other bank equipment.

A youth of about 15 approached a man observing the looting scene and said he needed a ride in order to take a stolen bank computer home. The man refused.

A man pulled up in a well-worn VW bus with his wife and a couple of small children. The woman jumped from the bus, ran into a liquor store that was being looted and returned a short time later carrying several bottles of wine.

The opportunities at this shopping center proved a strong lure for many—blacks, Latinos and a sprinkling of young whites. There were families as well as individuals. Men and women. The very young and the very old.

LEE HARRIS
Times staff writer

led to job loss, the aerospace industry is losing jobs and there is a flight of industry from California."

Political activist Kerman Maddox headed over to KGFJ, a black-owned radio station on La Brea where he worked part time as a broadcaster. At Jefferson and Western, people shouted "Let's rush Boys!" and a crowd of 50 to 75 people suddenly ran into the Boys market and cleared the shelves. All over La Brea, people were running. Trash cans were on fire, businesses in flames. The riots were moving west and north. Maddox reached the station and went on the air, but with a feeling of bitter irony. Here he was, a man with solid links to community and church and the political Establishment, the institutions that made the world work. Here he was, on the radio, telling people to stay cool. And outside, glowing embers were drifting toward the palm trees nearby. "I don't know how much longer we'll be on the air," he murmured, "because directly across the street from us, there is a fire raging out of control." Maddox could hear explosions coming from the inferno. Firetrucks roared up. The city was burning. Electrical power was out in parts of town. People were dying in the streets.

This wasn't America, Maddox thought. This was like the Middle East.

As fires blazed across Los Angeles, Mark Garcia was drawn to the flames. Curiosity lured the gangly 15-year-old, friends said, to a burning mini-mall at Hawthorne Boulevard and 101st Street. There was looting, but Garcia did not participate, friends said. Sure, he had hung around with some gangbangers, his mother would say later, but he stayed out of trouble. He lived with his mother and an 18-year-old brother in a converted garage. Moody and quiet, he wanted to be an architect. Or a cop.

Suddenly, a group of sheriff's deputies arrived at the mini-mall. They said they chased four jewelry store looters fleeing in a black Ford Tempo. Shots were fired, then the alleged looters jumped out of their car. The deputies caught up with them in a parking lot and returned fire. Garcia ended up dead.

Like so many deaths during the riots, the precise circumstances of this one were murky. The Sheriff's Department initially reported that Garcia had been in the fleeing car. Later, they said he was already in the parking lot when the car screeched to a halt. They said they shot him as he scaled a fence with another youth who was firing at them. But no gun or booty was found on Garcia.

n big and small ways, the rioting was disrupting lives. Government offices, courthouses, libraries, banks, big companies and shopping malls shut down. Hourlong lines formed at supermarkets and gas stations as residents stocked up. Mail delivery was suspended in 14 hard-hit ZIP codes. Professional baseball and basketball games were canceled. The utility company told one South Los Angeles woman it was too dangerous to send out a repairman to fix a power outage so her husband's kidney dialysis machine would work. Eventually, paramedics provided a portable dialysis system.

By midafternoon, Blue Line train operators could barely see through the smoke along Washington Boulevard, so passengers were loaded onto buses.

Looting that had gone virtually unchecked early in the rioting got more attention from authorities as the second day of unrest wore on. This man fled empty-handed from a sporting goods store at Vermont and 1st Street after being warned by on-lookers that police were on their way.

Photo: Gerard Burkhart

Two California Highway Patrol officers stand guard near the Westside after the unrest spread beyond South Los Angeles. In the background, taggers offered their thoughts on "the solution."

Photo: Jim Mendenhall

Stranded commuters were seen hitchhiking on freeways. Transit officials announced that all bus service would be suspended at 6 p.m. The city school district extended its closings to include every school and child-care center. At the University of Southern California, final examinations were postponed and frightened students fled for family homes. "Everybody's really nervous," said Kacy O'Brien as she and fellow members of the Kappa Kappa Gamma sorority hurriedly departed from Greek Row. "We're getting out of here."

Hundreds of National Guardsmen, meanwhile, took up positions in hot spots. Armed with loaded M-16 rifles and riding in armored cars, they stationed themselves behind the police to help secure areas from looters and arsonists. In some areas, the soldiers were welcomed. But many were heckled and taunted. Some appeared jittery, including a few who had served in the Persian Gulf War. "This is a lot different from attacking an Iraqi bunker," Col. Roger Goodrich said. "There you know who the enemy is....This is citizen soldiers facing citizens."

Near the Los Angeles Memorial Coliseum, where three fires burned heavily and a man had recently been shot, Staff Sgt. Jack Nix took up position in front of a graffiti-covered wall that bore the message: "This is for Rodney King." A 19-year Guard veteran and a military police officer by profession, Nix found his new duty unsettling. As ashes fell like snow on his helmet, he confided frankly, "It's scary, absolutely scary."

The guardsmen were late. There had been an embarrassing glitch. A communications breakdown and ammunition shortage had kept them cooling their heels in armories for most of the day. Local authorities and Guard commanders had been unable to agree on where to send them. Then, their extra ammunition had been delayed; no one had given the order to ship it. "This ammunition problem should not have occurred," Gov. Wilson said in a late-afternoon news conference. "It will not again."

Warren Christopher drove home from his office Thursday afternoon. Fires seemed to be everywhere, the National Guard nowhere. The 66-year-old chairman of the citizens' commission that had been appointed to investigate police operations after the King beating began to wonder if the city did not have enough law enforcement forces. At home, Christopher decided reluctantly to intervene.

He called the mayor. He urged him to alert federal officials that the city might need federal troops. Christopher had been through it before, as a deputy attorney general in the U.S. Department of Justice during riots in Detroit and Chicago in the late 1960's. Bradley mulled over the suggestion, then authorized Christopher to handle the request. He spent the evening on the phone to Washington.

What was occurring was far more severe than what Christopher had expected. The Police Department's top management clearly had been in disarray. The department was in flux, with Gates' top aides on vacation, retiring or not on speaking terms with the chief. The people Gates had relied on to run the department were unavailable to help manage this crisis, Christopher thought. There was a crucial gap in leadership at a critical time. "I was also not aware that the mayor and the police chief had not been speaking to each other for a year,"

THURSDAY, APRIL 30, 4:30 P.M.
Martin Luther King Boulevard
and Vermont Avenue

Staff Sgt. John Nix was one of the first National Guardsmen to hit the streets of Los Angeles. His unit took up position at the corner of Martin Luther King Boulevard and Vermont Avenue about 4 p.m. Thursday. Buildings were burning all around. Police were few and far between.

Within an hour, a man was shot in the arm just a few yards away. Nix helped administer first aid, then returned to his corner.

"This is bad," he said, looking up and down the boulevard. "And when it gets dark, it gets much worse."

JIM NEWTON
Times staff writer

Officers stand ready as fire units battle a blaze near 19th Street and Adams Boulevard. Police officials claimed that deployment of patrols to protect firefighting units restricted their ability to counter the violence that quickly spread beyond downtown and South Los Angeles.

Photo: Patrick Downs

Hundreds of men and women are looting a Tianguis supermarket. People running through aisles, knocking things off the shelves, loading their arms with groceries.

In the panic to get away quickly, the looters have dropped dozens of milk cartons, bags of flour, tomatoes and oranges along the aisles and through the entrances, creating a slippery mush. A man running out loses his balance, his feet rising comically in the air as he tumbles to the ground.

Outside, in the parking lot, photographer Larry Davis and I are taking it all in. A teen-ager standing in the parking lot yells at me. "Hey you! Who are you? What are you writing?"

"I'm from the L.A. Times," I answer. "The newspaper."

Another looter grabs my notebook, checking to see what I am writing. Suddenly I understand—they are afraid I'm copying car license plate numbers. Larry keeps snapping pictures. An orange comes flying in our direction. It misses by a mile, but we get the point anyway. Time to leave. As we walk briskly away, another orange passes over us. Then, as I am opening the car door, a gallon-size jug of milk explodes at my feet.

"Call the police! Call the police!" a man yells in an Armenian accent as we drive away. Several people standing by him smile and laugh. The police are nowhere to be found.

HECTOR TOBAR
Times staff writer

Christopher said later.

Looting continued to spread during the afternoon through Watts and Compton, along the Mid-Wilshire corridor and into Westwood. Crowds charged up Hollywood Boulevard, stealing everything they could lay their hands on, including a bustier from Frederick's of Hollywood said to have been worn by Madonna. "The problem is widening, intensifying," Police Commission President Sheinbaum warned as dusk approached. "You have a whole social upheaval."

n Long Beach, Matt Haines and Scott Coleman set out on a motorcycle at about 6 p.m. A friend, a black woman, had called asking for help in packing so she could leave the riot area. Haines was an auto mechanic—age 32, white, with a free-spirited, generous streak. Coleman, 26, was his nephew, close friend and roommate. After they set off, the woman tried to warn them not to come; the rioting was growing fierce. But it was too late. A mob of black men and teen-agers surrounded the motorcycle. "Hey, we're on your side," objected Haines. But the group knocked the men to the ground and beat them. Then one man took out a gun, slid the barrel under Haines' helmet and shot him dead. Turning to Coleman, he shot him three times in the arm. But when he pointed the gun at Coleman's face and pulled the trigger, the gun didn't fire. It had either jammed or run out of bullets. "Had they bothered to even speak with him, they would have found out they didn't need to kill him," Haines' sister, Cris Baldwin, said later. "There's no one in our family who didn't think the King verdict was wrong."

Just before curfew, hundreds of looters swept along 3rd and Bonnie Brae streets in Los Angeles, raiding a Tianguis market and fleeing with armloads of stolen groceries. For some, it got messy, even dangerous. Several lost their footing on floors slick with flour and crushed tomatoes, spilling their booty. "Free food! Free food in there!" was the shout as they fled. Onlookers could not resist the offer. One teen-age reveler said he had driven from Santa Monica for a piece of the action. "I don't even believe it myself," he said.

In Koreatown, the California Market had come through Wednesday night intact, barricaded with pallets of rice and cabbage, 20 armed employees out front. But by Thursday afternoon, looting raged all around. A fire broke out at a mini-mall half a block away. Then shooting began. The first carload of rioters was repulsed with a burst of gunfire into the air. Then came a second, then a third carload of shooters. Late in the evening, another shop owner called: A carload of looters was heading their way. It was a false alarm. The night then settled into an uneasy calm. The guards on the roof came down to the cartridge-strewn parking lot to drink soda and eat pastry.

A short distance away, Edward Song Lee had answered a call for help from another embattled merchant. An 18-year-old college freshman, he had been raised traditionally and his parents still lived in Koreatown. At about 10:30 p.m., shooting broke out. In the cross-fire of bullets fired by looters, security guards and police, Lee collapsed onto the pavement and died in an expanding stain of blood. It was unclear who shot Lee, except that officials said it was not a police officer. "He felt

A loot-ladened woman makes her way through a ransacked market at 3rd and Catalina streets during the second day of rioting following the King verdicts. When questioned, many looters said they felt they had a right to their stolen merchandise.

Photo: Larry Davis

Rioters smashed windows and looted
Frederick's of Hollywood on
Hollywood Boulevard.

Photo: Gary Friedman

it was his responsibility to protect other Koreans who could not defend themselves," his mother, Jung Hui Lee, later said. "If he didn't feel so strongly about being a responsible Korean, he would be alive."

Outside of the city, the anarchy was proving contagious. Long Beach declared a state of emergency. In Riverside County, fires roared. And a security guard killed a 17-year-old man when 50 looters stormed a San Bernardino discount outlet.

In San Francisco, marauding youths smashed windows, set small fires and raided some of the city's most elegant boutiques. Union Square, the city's beloved shopping district, was littered with glass, debris and an occasional stolen tennis shoe. Guests at the elegant St. Francis Hotel watched from the lobby. "Why should people go around wrecking things for no reason?" wondered a bewildered Bob Appleton, vacationing with his family from The Hague, Netherlands. The bell captain at another hotel said unnerved guests had "broken down and cried."

In downtown Atlanta, hundreds of black youths went on a rampage. In Madison, Wis., the windshields of 34 parked police cars were shattered. "Justice for King," read a note at the scene. In New York City, students at a Catholic school in Queens walked out of their classes chanting "Rodney, Rodney, Rodney." In Providence, R.I., and Seattle, city officials and black community leaders appealed for calm. In Washington, D.C., all police officers' leaves were canceled and units were put on alert in anticipation of trouble.

Back in South-Central Los Angeles, Nettie Lewis' family sat on their front porch in the dark and watched flames on the horizon. High above, the governor of California took a helicopter tour of the perimeter of the troubled area. The noise was relentless—sirens, sporadic gunfire, helicopters overhead. Lewis' 3-year-old granddaughter fell asleep with her hands pressed against her ears.

All across the city, frightened and bewildered children tried to make sense of what was happening. They congregated on street corners in inner-city neighborhoods, watching buildings burn. Eleven-year-old Licette Hernandez stood in front of the Paradise Funeral Home near 52nd Street and Broadway, clutching her sides as firefighters fought a furniture store fire. "I'm scared of all of this," she said. "My stomach hurts. It's been hurting since last night when my dad didn't come home until midnight. My mother was desperate. Black people were running in the street screaming 'Rodney King! Rodney King!' "

Jose Soto, an 11-year-old sixth-grader at 52nd Street School, watched a fire burning behind the rented house where he lived with his mother and brother. He saw looters in the corner thrift store. His parents assured him everything would be cleaned up. "I would like to move to some clean place. Far from here," Soto said. "Right here is terrible. There's no more stores or anything. It's wrong. Because this is where we live, this is where we're supposed to get our food and everything. It's not fair."

In Simi Valley, Steve and Leslie Frank debated whether to allow their 12-year-old twins to watch the televised violence. Leslie left the TV on. They were old

THURSDAY, APRIL 30, 2 P.M.
Vermont Avenue and 3rd Street

Rioters had just broken into a Thrifty's and other stores on the east side of Vermont. Gunshots could be heard. Korean merchants stood their ground. On the west side of the street, buildings were engulfed in flames, and firefighters and police swarmed this way and that trying to control the crowds and the flames.

In the middle of it all, and seemingly oblivious, was Tom Ramos, his shoulders hunched over, staring blankly at the gutted remains of the old apartment complex on West 3rd Street. Ramos, 57, had lived in the building for the past 13 years, and had spent the morning watching his life go up in flames. "I lost everything," he said slowly, not taking his eyes off his old apartment. "Now I have to start all over again."

For the next hour or so, as I continued my work, I would occasionally glance back at Ramos—still there, motionless, staring at his former home.

Jim Davids, a grizzled Los Angeles County firefighter with a face blackened by soot, leaned against his hook-and-ladder and watched Ramos from afar.

"It's insanity," he said, shaking his head slowly. "It just isn't fair."

JOSH MEYER
Times staff writer

A National Guardsman hunkered down as shots were fired at 6th Street and Western Avenue. Authorities reported sniper fire throughout the unrest. Before the rioting would end, a guardsman would shoot and kill a Latino who allegedly tried twice to drive his beat-up Datsun through Guard barricades at Pico and Vermont. It was the only use of deadly force by a guardsman during the unrest.

Photo: J. Albert Diaz

Edward Song Lee, 18, foreground, was shot to death and three other Koreans were injured in an exchange of gunfire with looters at 3rd and Hobart streets in Koreatown during the second night of violence. Police officers questioned the survivors of the attack, who were shot while trying to protect a Korean-owned pizza parlor.

enough, she figured, and they would inherit the problems. But the girls were confused. How do you explain to them that somebody is stealing a TV from a Fedco discount store because of the jury's decision, Steve Frank wondered. If you find it difficult to explain to an adult, how do you explain it to your kids?

They tried to tell the children that no matter how frustrated you are, violence and destruction do not solve things. They also defended the jury's decision. "Looters and criminals should have no excuses made for them," said Steve Frank. "These people who are out there blaming it on Reagan… have to take responsibilities for themselves. And they don't like it. They're trying to blame someone else for their problems."

Unemployed child-care worker Laura Price, too, tried to explain the terror to two teen-age nephews who had come to stay with her in South Los Angeles because their home was in the midst of rioting. Society has a dominant group, Price told them, which feels superior. Rodney King wasn't beaten for doing something bad, she said; he was beaten because white cops caught him in a white neighborhood. "I also told them, no matter what white people are saying, we are not a lesser race. Behind every successful white man there's a black man. I'm from the South, and I've seen them take blacks' ideas and claim it for themselves, whether it's music or literature."

There were moments, watching the violence on television, when Price thought that this time, if there was to be looting and burning, let it be in white communities. Not hers. "A small part of me felt like, 'Yeah, hit that one.' When I realized it had gotten to the San Fernando Valley, I said, 'Yes! Don't just tear up our neighborhood. Go out there where people have money to fix it.' Then I realized what I was feeling, and I reprimanded myself."

Shortly before midnight, Mayor Bradley and Gov. Wilson announced they had requested more National Guard troops, bringing the total to 6,000. The U.S. military, too, had been asked to go on alert. As the second day of rioting ended, the official toll of destruction had soared: Twenty-five deaths, 572 injuries, hundreds of fires and arrests, and $200 million to $250 million in estimated damage.

THURSDAY, APRIL 30, 2:45 P.M.
Southbound Amtrak train

The San Diegan normally carries about 100 people heading southbound out of Union Station to Orange County and beyond. On this most unusual of days there were 200 extra riders, including myself, escaping Los Angeles early.

Although many of us felt safe at our workplace downtown, nearly everyone talked of husbands or wives, mothers and fathers who pleaded with us not to work at all. Our compromise was to leave early.

We headed home to peaceful neighborhoods with much of a sunny day ahead. But the train was somber.

I heard later that the impression was people in Orange County went along with business as usual. Perhaps we continued to work out, go surfing and shop, but at the gym, beach and mall the horror of Los Angeles was on everyone's lips and minds. Never did 50 miles seem so distant and yet so close.

SHERRY STERN
TV Times editor

In churches and homes throughout Los Angeles, people prayed and pleaded for peace while violence reigned outside. Sandra Evers-Manlcy, president of the Beverly Hills-Hollywood NAACP, is solemn as a nearby building burns.

Photo: Gary Friedman

6

"...CAN WE GET ALONG?"

FRIDAY, MAY 1, 1992

On the third day, Rodney King came out of hiding. He emerged from his lawyer's office in Beverly Hills to be engulfed by a throng of 100 reporters. City Hall had called minutes earlier: King wouldn't say or do anything to make the situation worse, would he? the mayor's staff wanted to know. Nervous and barely audible, his voice lost at times to the blast of helicopter rotors overhead, King delivered a halting plea for peace that, in its rambling, elliptical, tragic quality, became one of the more memorable moments in the Los Angeles riots.

"Can we get along?" King asked, almost begging. "Can we stop making it horrible for the older people and the kids?... We've got enough smog here in Los Angeles, let alone to deal with the setting of these fires and things. It's just not right. It's not right, and it's not going to change anything. We'll get our justice. They've won the battle, but they haven't won the war. We will have our day in court, and that's all we want.... I'm neutral. I love everybody. I love people of color.... I'm not like they're... making me out to be.

"We've got to quit. We've got to quit.... I can understand the first upset in for the first two hours after the verdict, but to go on, to keep going on like this, and to see a the security guard shot on the ground, it's just not right. It's just not right because those people will never go home to their families again. And I mean, please, we can get along here. We all can get along. We've just got to, just got to. We're all stuck here for a while....Let's try to work it out. Let's try to work it out."

Eight hours earlier, before dawn, it was decided that federal forces would be sent to Los Angeles. Between 1:15 a.m. and 5:30 a.m., Gov. Wilson and Mayor Bradley conferred with Washington. At 7:15 a.m., officials announced that President Bush would send in 1,000 federal agents—including 200 members of the U.S. marshal's special operations group that was sent to Panama in 1990 to take dictator Manuel Noriega into custody. Federal and local officials said the muscle-flexing, called long overdue by many in ransacked areas of the city, was meant to "ensure the safety of the streets" before the weekend.

The overnight curfew left the smoldering city in a nervous calm. Streets were almost deserted, as were restaurants, theaters and sporting arenas. In some areas, only the homeless remained outdoors. Thick smoke still hung over much of the Los Angeles Basin, fires burned from Hollywood to South Los Angeles, and new outbreaks of violence erupted in Long Beach, the Harbor area, Mid-City and in the San Fernando Valley community of Panorama City.

A city that had long boasted about its Third-World flavor was beginning to mirror the worst of its war-torn neighbors to the south: Military equipment rolled down boulevards, men with automatic weapons stood sentry. Long-overdue National Guard units took back pieces of the city Friday. But their welcome was soured by

FRIDAY, MAY 1, 2:30 P.M.
Vermont and Manchester avenues

A single tear is rolling down the right cheek of Norman Simples, a burly black man in jeans and a bulletproof vest. He has just returned to his business, the Commercial SkyPager, to find it looted and burned, despite the spray-painted letters that said "Black Owned."

Simples and his employees—armed with rifles and semiautomatic guns—had guarded it successfully for two nights, but left when the National Guard arrived. His lament was as much about the Guard's failure as it was about black life in Los Angeles: "All it is is building up our hopes for something," he said. "Always building up our hopes for something, to let us down."

SHERYL STOLBERG
Times staff writer

After two days of violence that rocked the city and the nation, Rodney King, the motorist whose beating led to the trial in Simi Valley, broke his long silence in the case. He asked, almost pleaded, that the killing, looting and destruction be stopped.

Photo: Larry Davis

angry residents who had lost their neighborhoods while snafus delayed their deployment. "How could it take them so long?" asked a crying Nargas Nadjati, a South-Central resident who arrived at her brother's grocery store to find nothing but wreckage. "They are so fast to send troops to the other side of the world. Why can't they save our city?"

The Guard's first load of ammunition and body armor, it turned out, arrived in Los Angeles hours late. Though Wilson called up the units Wednesday evening, it was not until daybreak Thursday that a Guard helicopter picked up the ammunition—including "lock plates" to convert the guardsmen's M-16 automatic weapons to semiautomatic—at Camp Roberts, a training base outside of Paso Robles. The helicopter had been unable to load at night, officials explained, because Camp Roberts lacked lights on its Tarmac. So the equipment reached Los Angeles 17 hours after the call-up. "I think it is an outrage that [they] showed up without ammunition," said state Controller Gray Davis, vowing to investigate. "That's like the Dodgers taking the field without their gloves."

Where the Guard was in place, the ranks were sometimes stretched perilously thin. Young soldiers worried that they could not hold some areas with so few people. Beleaguered shopkeepers complained bitterly when the guardsmen were reassigned to new locations, leaving residents to fend for themselves. At one Ralph's supermarket, looting raged for hours before Guard units moved in Friday morning. As the units looked on, cleanup crews scooped mounds of spilled food off the floor and boarded up shattered windows. Then, in early afternoon, the guardsmen were called away. The looters began to circle again. One man even brought a shopping cart. "I don't know why they don't keep at least 10 [guardsmen] out here," said Joel Lopez, the owner of a gold-trading store across the street. "See that guy with the shopping cart? They're going to tear this right back down and go in."

Myung Lee had been too frightened to return to her South Los Angeles doughnut shop on Thursday. When she went back Friday, she found it looted. The plate-glass windows were shattered, the cash register was gone, not a single doughnut was left. She stood in a corner of the mini-mall and cried: "I hate this business…. I hate it!" A few minutes later, her spirits lifted. A few Latino residents arrived with brooms and trash bags to help clean up the stores in the mall. Neither Lee nor her neighbor, William Hong, realized they were the same people who had done the looting. A couple of the women had injuries suffered during the rampage; in the rush to escape from the store, one had fallen on the broken glass. Leticia and Anna were among the group. Leticia was feeling guilty; Anna apologized to Hong.

"Chino, I was one of the people who took things from your store," she said. "I took 10 six-packs. I'm sorry, Chino. I'll pay you for the beer if you want." No, Hong said, he didn't want the money. He was grateful to Anna for saving the building from fire. They exchanged phone numbers and Anna agreed to call him at home if somebody again tried to burn the store. Later, three soldiers took up positions in front of the video store. The women in the apartment complex gave them water and quesadillas. One guardsman politely knocked on Anna and

Leticia's door. His six-foot frame barely fit into the tiny apartment. The soldier asked for another glass of water. Anna was more than happy to oblige. "Since the National Guard is here, we feel better," she said. "We're against violence."

If one street defined the destruction, Vermont Avenue was it. It seemed to personify the city's broken spirit. For 10 miles between Santa Monica Boulevard in Hollywood and Manchester Boulevard in South-Central Los Angeles, it had become a holocaust of fire-gutted buildings and shattered glass. Block after block, people's lives had been ripped apart. A 71-year-old man, burned out of his apartment, was now homeless. Three Los Angeles police officers had been shot there early Friday, although none was seriously injured. Uninsured business owners, many of them immigrants who had come to the United States in search of promise and dreams, had lost everything. The devastation slashed through racial lines: a Filipino-owned camera shop, a Korean-owned furniture store, a Latino-owned restaurant, a black-owned telephone pager business.

At Santa Monica Boulevard stood the hulking, twisted wreckage of what had been a Payless shoe store. A hundred yards away, there was an attempt at order: Armed employees stood guard at the Hollytron electronics and appliance store, fending off any would-be intruders. With rifles and binoculars, they had been there since the rioting began. Early Friday, before they took up their posts in the parking lot and on the roof, they prayed for peace.

South along the avenue, Simon Ong studied the charred remains of the camera shop he had owned for 17 years. He could barely speak. He estimated that he had suffered $1 million in losses from the blaze, set Thursday evening after he left to get chains to secure the building. His employees had not found out about the fire until they arrived for work Friday. Half a dozen of them milled about the parking lot in a daze, some sifting through the ashes. Edwin Castro, 25, wrung his blackened hands and moaned: "Man, I just want my job."

At the Goldilocks Bakeshop and Restaurant, in a mini-mall of Filipino-owned shops at 3rd Street and Vermont, manager Raul Maguddayao counted his blessings. Before him, a display case of the bakery's specialties was in shambles. Tiny plastic adornments—flowers, Easter bunnies, colored flags—were littered about. Shelves of white sheet cakes had collapsed. "We were not hurt as much as the others," Maguddayao said optimistically, as workers scraped up glass. "I'm glad we're not burned. I'm thankful for that."

Plywood was in big demand. Vermont and Rosewood Avenue: Windows at the California Highway Patrol headquarters were boarded up. Vermont and Beverly Boulevard: More plywood, resting against an office building that was waiting for repairs. Vermont and Council Street: Two men nailed boards to the Lifetime Furniture store. In the Mid-Wilshire District, hardly a block along Vermont went unscathed. If there was a bright spot, it was that cleanup crews were in high gear, many from local churches. They were a sign of hope amid the decay.
On block after burned-out block from the Fairfax District to Crenshaw Boulevard, from Leimert Park to Western Avenue, volunteers ventured forth Friday with tangible symbols of their commitment—shovels, brooms, water hoses, trash

FRIDAY, MAY 1, 9 A.M.
First A.M.E. Church, Mid-City

In the wake of the riots, political candidates were quick to make inquiries about touring devastated areas.

I was in the office of First A.M.E. pastor Cecil L. (Chip) Murray when former Gov. Edmund G. (Jerry) Brown called twice to ask the best time to visit.

Murray, whose church had become a central gathering spot and disaster relief site, put Brown on the speaker phone.

Both times, the Democratic presidential candidate proceeded to debate with himself whether he should come when other public officials were there or arrive later. And both times, Brown launched into long monologues that sounded like his stump campaign speech.

During the second call, a fidgety Murray looked out the window and eyed the Rev. Jesse Jackson alighting from a car.

"Jerry," said the pastor, "your vice president has just arrived. I've got to go."

PAUL FELDMAN
Times staff writer

After lengthy delays, hundreds of National Guardsmen loaded with M-16 rifles and riding in armored cars took up positions in hot spots around the city. These guardsmen patrolled the area near Martin Luther King Boulevard and Vermont Avenue as a mini-mall went up in flames.

Photo: Lori Shepler

containers. African-Americans, Anglos and Latinos working together temporarily put aside their pain and outrage over the wanton destruction, taking to the streets to reclaim their neighborhoods. "Just a year ago, I was in the cleanup in Kuwait and Saudi Arabia," said Chad Mac, a 19-year-old Marine whose mother lived in the neighborhood he was helping clean up. "Now you have to turn around and do the same thing in your own back yard. It's sad."

Cars cruised Vermont. Many occupants waved, honked horns and gave the peace sign to those cleaning up. At a mini-mall where several shops had been gutted, a truck pulled up carrying 15 UCLA students who went to work with brooms and shovels. They were joined by another group that included Elmore Dingle, 31. "I especially wanted to help the Koreans," said Dingle, a black man. "I don't want them to think so negatively about blacks. The violence last night wasn't real. This is real." Residents of View Park, Baldwin Hills and Leimert Park tackled a block of Degnan Boulevard best known for its black art galleries, jazz performance space and theater complex. "I was watching TV and feeling helpless when I saw [actor] Edward James Olmos leading a cleanup on Western Avenue," said Jack Roberts, a retired human resources manager for First Interstate Bank. "I thought that was a darned good idea. It gets rid of this helpless feeling."

Olmos was striding down Western Avenue Friday morning like a man possessed. "Pick up everything!" he exhorted a volunteer cleanup brigade he was leading. Rocker Tom Petty recorded a song, "Peace in LA," to be rushed to local radio stations that night. Arsenio Hall, the television talk show host, visited children at a Red Cross shelter and took part in a nationally broadcast radio call-in show. From Warner Bros. studio in Burbank to South Los Angeles, the entertainment community responded to Mayor Bradley's calls for support. Said choreographer Debbie Allen at a star rally on a Warner Bros. sound stage, "Let's not polarize our community any further."

Normal life, nevertheless, remained in suspension. Panic buying spread through food stores all over Southern California. Armored cars couldn't make it to many local banks. As tumult and fear gummed up distribution networks, things as basic as buying gasoline became an impossibility in parts of Los Angeles. Supermarkets ran out of food staples, mail deliveries were cut. Businesses missed their payrolls and deadlines. "There's no place to shop, no phone, no place to get medicine," said Evelyn Jones, 31, who lives on 103rd Place between Central and Century Boulevard. "...It's like a war zone. As soon as the sun goes down, out come the guns."

At Broadway and West 88th Place, scores of mothers with small children waited in line for hours at the Broadway Station post office. Many were hoping to collect their first-of-the-month welfare checks—though they also noted that banks were closed and the closest check-cashing service was in ashes. Adding to the misery was that homes near the center of the uprising were without electricity. Officials of the Department of Water and Power said that about 21,000 homes still

FRIDAY, MAY 1, 1:30 P.M.
Broadway Avenue and West 85th,
South Los Angeles

A mass of people, mostly women with children, wait in the midday sun to collect their mail at the Broadway Station post office. An army of sheriff's deputies and LAPD officers watch from the middle of the street, rifles at the ready.

Mothers tell of their desperation. There's no place left to cash the first-of-the-month government checks that they're waiting for. Neighborhood food stores smolder in ashes. Fires have knocked out electricity and with it, refrigerators. Old women crumple from exhaustion. Babies wail. Here are some of the riot's worst victims.

"Everything is burned out," says Loletta Lewis, 34. "We need candles, batteries and flashlights." Nearby, Janice Walker holds her 8-month-old boy, Nathaniel James Walker.

"I need juice and Pampers," Walker says. "I am out of food." At that point, LAPD Officer Kirk Hunter apparently overhears and hands Nathaniel his one small squeeze carton of Tang.

"I've got kids," Hunter, who is white, tells me later. "I understand how they feel out here. I wish I could give everybody juice."

DAVID WILLMAN
Times staff writer

The unrest took a heavy toll on businesses throughout South Los Angeles. Isaac Suthers, co-owner of Jazz Etc., said "people come up and cry" when they see that the popular year-old night spot was gutted by fire.

Photo: Gary Friedman

lacked power and that repair work was delayed by the need to wait for police escorts.

The despair was palpable inside the post office, where those fortunate enough to collect their checks had other misfortunes to contend with. "Everything around me is destroyed," said 43-year-old Brenda Hollins. "They stole my car from Broadway and Central. The same thugs that are burning and looting stole my car. I had to walk all the way from 76th and Avalon to get here." Janice Walker, holding her 8-month-old son, Nathaniel, said she feared that the community's suffering would get worse. "I need juice and Pampers," Walker said. "I am out of food."

"It's horrible what they've done," said Adey Behre, a 37-year-old parking lot attendant, referring to looters and vandals who ravaged stores near her apartment on South Fairfax Avenue near Pico Boulevard. "I'm from Ethiopia, where they have a lot of problems. But I've never seen anything like this."

Yet for every horror story, there seemed to be a tale of neighborliness or heroism. Not all of them, however, had happy endings. In Inglewood, a 24-year-old good Samaritan died trying to save a burning store near his home. Kevin Evanshen plunged through a weakened roof on Inglewood Boulevard while helping put out flames in a looted check-cashing store. He had climbed a ladder onto the single-story roof to pour water through a burning hole when the roof collapsed.

Meanwhile, federal involvement in the crisis widened. Bradley announced that the state would seek an official federal disaster declaration. And in a nationally televised, prime-time address from the Oval Office, Bush announced that he was dispatching 4,500 federal troops to Los Angeles. The 1,500 Marines and 3,000 soldiers would be assisted by 1,000 federal agents—including FBI SWAT teams, U.S. marshals and special border patrol units—sent to Los Angeles earlier in the day. Bush vowed to use "whatever force is necessary to restore order" if violence were to flare anew.

Bush also announced that a federal grand jury had already issued subpoenas as part of an accelerated Justice Department investigation into whether the beating of Rodney King violated federal civil rights laws. White House aides described the unusual disclosure as an attempt by Bush to soothe the destructive anger sparked by the not-guilty verdicts. "Viewed from outside the trial, it was hard to understand how the verdict could possibly square with the video," Bush said, sounding his strongest note of empathy to date for those outraged by the verdict. He said he was stunned. "And so was Barbara, and so were my kids."

Two full days of chaos were taking a toll on city institutions. Hospitals, in particular, showed the strain. About 83 hospitals reported treating people for riot-related injuries—bullet and knife wounds, cuts, broken bones. Supplies dwindled and fatigue set in. The hardest-hit hospitals were reported to be practicing battlefield medicine. Though the stream of injured had begun to slow, some hospitals found themselves inundated with a new wave of sick people who had postponed hospital visits scheduled for earlier in the week.

Impassable streets, fires and violence interfered with deliveries of medical supplies. The police had ferried blood to Martin Luther King Jr./Drew Medical

OPPOSITE
A young boy checks out the firepower of a Marine guard stationed in front of a Boy's market in Compton. That city was particularly hard hit by rioters: All but two of its dozen or so grocery stores were reduced to ashes.

Photo: Larry Davis

Center in Watts on Thursday. Los Angeles County-USC Medical Center in Boyle Heights dedicated five operating rooms around the clock to riot victims, a spokesman said. Patients streamed in on their own or with the help of passersby.

J ails, too, were overloaded. As crackdowns began, the county's already-groaning criminal justice bureaucracy braced for an avalanche. Los Angeles police were under orders to arrest rioters "for the most serious crime evident;" the district attorney's office announced that it would file the harshest charges legally possible. The upshot: By late Friday, the official number of riot-related arrests countywide was approaching 5,200. In some areas, suspects were being taken into custody a dozen or more at a time. It was standing room only Friday afternoon at the Hawthorne City Jail. In Inglewood, 130 people were jammed into a slammer built for 29. The county's big Central Jail was faring slightly better—it still had a few hundred spaces left by dusk. But bunks were going fast.

Special sheriff's teams were dispatched to book suspects in the field, taking their mug shots and fingerprints before shipping them by the busload to the County Jail. About 600 convicted felons in the county system awaiting transport to state prison were hustled off early to make room for new arrestees. The Los Angeles Municipal Court downtown announced it would reopen for the weekend to handle the arraignment rush. And, just in case things got too heavy, the state Supreme Court extended the usual 48-hour deadline for filing formal charges against arrestees to 96 hours. "We're bursting," said Lt. Richard Didion, watch commander of the inmate reception center at Central Jail. "This place is really bulging, and we don't know how many more we'll have."

With order returning to the streets Friday afternoon, Charles (Sticks) Orebo and two friends, Andre Webb and Lavelle (Frog) Williams, discussed shooting some hoops the following morning. The curfew was approaching, so the trio drove toward South Los Angeles. Near an intersection on Florence Avenue, Orebo tried to make a lane change and nearly cut off a blue Camaro behind him. The other driver honked and pulled alongside at a stoplight. Williams drew a handgun, loaded a clip, and pointed the gun across Orebo's face toward the other driver—a Los Angeles police officer named Brian Liddy, out of uniform and en route to work. "The guy looked at us," recalled Webb, "and he jumped like he was in shock. Then he pulled up his gun.... Then he shot like three times and hit Sticks."

Orebo, struck by the gunfire, punched the accelerator. The car lurched into a wall and moments later caught fire. Williams began firing at Liddy. An off-duty sheriff's deputy came to Liddy's aid. Webb and Williams fled on foot but were arrested. Orebo, a high school dropout with a 4-year-old son, died. He had planned to get married the following month and become an auto mechanic. He had been jailed a couple times for traffic tickets and other small offenses, his mother later said. "But nothing violent. No guns or anything like that.... From what I gathered, my son didn't know [Williams] had the gun until he pulled it up. I'm angry, but I'm angry with the young man."

Once again, the curfew descended. The streets emptied and grew quiet.

FRIDAY, MAY 1, 10:30 A.M.
East 66th Street, South Los Angeles

As fellow staff writer Fred Muir and I pulled up to a house, hoping to interview the family of one of the first people killed in the riots, we noticed five young men dressed like gang members congregated near the front door. One was sitting on a stereo boombox.

"Let's kick these white boys' asses," he said as we got out and approached them.

As calmly as I could, I explained who we were and what our mission was. They seemed to relax a little, but not much. They all seemed to know the deceased person—"You mean my homeboy?"—but insisted that he didn't live there.

"This is *East* 66th," they said, "you want *West* 66th."

As we retreated to the car, all I could think about was how ridiculous the whole experience had been, how we nearly got attacked for showing up at the wrong address.

DAVID FREED
Times staff writer

As tho toll from the rioting grew, more and more residents began taking to the streets to urge calm and work for peace. Bobby Wade shook hands with a like-minded motorist on Pico Boulevard and Fairfax Avenue, the scene of looting the night before.

Photo: Marilyn Weiss

Merchants anguished over the deepening cost. Wolfgang Puck's four trendy restaurants—Spago, Eureka, Chinois and Granita—had been closed Thursday night. Only Granita, in Malibu, was open Friday. The closures, to comply with the curfew, were expected to cost the eateries between $40,000 and $50,000 in gross sales per day. Restaurants, retailers and service enterprises could expect a continuing slump as long as the curfew, or just plain fear, kept people from venturing out.

Throughout the county, economists and business leaders were calculating the riots' impact on the recession-racked Southern California economy. Thousands of businesses, large and small, had been burned, looted or destroyed. Many would not be rebuilt. With more than $500 million in property damage alone, reconstruction would be daunting. The damage, in addition to straining tight state and local budgets, would produce an immeasurable loss of jobs and income. Unemployment would rise. The region's recovery from recession could be pushed back to 1993.

Uncertainty about the region's stability and safety could delay investment. Some foreign investment had already been put on hold. One international commercial real estate brokerage said 80% of its proposed deals with investors in Asia and Europe had been suspended for at least two to three months. The decisions would affect more than $100 million worth of property in Los Angeles. Tourism, too, was going to suffer. Japan's largest travel agency had already canceled tours, resulting in the loss of 1,200 tourists. At least one major convention was canceled.

The construction trades, which had collapsed with the real estate market, could expect only a mild boost repairing damaged buildings. Experience from past disasters, such as earthquakes, had shown that long-term economic damage more than offsets any temporary gain in construction business, experts said. Banks and other financial institutions would lose money. "Nearly every bank has some customers in the area that have been hurt, so they could face problem loans and loan losses," said Alexander Kyman, president and chairman of City National Bank.

Perhaps most damaging, the riots would certainly exacerbate the image of Los Angeles as a "Blade Runner" urban landscape of crime and decay. That image had already begun to overtake the palmier stereotypes of the past in many mass media reports, to the area's economic detriment.

John Hong spent Friday evening in Koreatown, guarding his father's store, Lucky Electronics, with nine other security guards. Be strong, the father had instructed his 16-year-old son. Don't do anything to hurt yourself because of the store; if we lose the stock, we'll rebuild. Hong answered, "Don't worry about anything." But he thought to himself: My dad's store is in our family's lifeline. If we lose this, we lose everything. It is my duty to go up there.

Hong thought he could understand what the looters were feeling. But looting was uncalled-for. He figured looters should get the death sentence. After all, they weren't looting people's stores, they were looting people's lives. It didn't seem to have much to do with Rodney King or Latasha Harlins, Hong thought. Sure, there had been problems between Korean and black parents. But before the

OPPOSITE
A child bows his head as family members are arrested for allegedly looting a store at the corner of Rodeo Road and La Cienega Boulevard.

Photo: Larry Davis

Authorities had their hands full handling the thousands of looters who descended upon stores throughout the area during the unrest. These Los Angeles County sheriff's deputies kept watch on a group of people arrested after a store on Martin Luther King Jr. Boulevard was looted.

Photo: Steve Dykes

John Matlock, 65, who had a job cleaning up at this shopping center in Leimert Park, was put out of work by the unrest, as were about 20,000 area workers. Officials estimated that thousands of those jobs might not return for a year or more.

Photo: Larry Bessel

riot, Hong himself was still making friends with black kids and Hispanic kids and any kids at Warren High School in Downey, where he was a sophomore.

"Now after the riot, some kids treat me differently," Hong would say later. "I treat them differently. We look at what happened in a different way. We're not as close as we were.... If there is any more controversy between the Korean community and black community, I feel we'll be just like the adults saying, 'You're bad' and 'No, *you're* bad.' "

Alberto Machon, a high school junior who had moved from El Salvador to South-Central Los Angeles 10 years earlier, laughed when he saw the Korean markets looted and burned. "I didn't pay no mind," he recalled. "...I didn't actually go in there and take something, but I didn't mind. At some point, I felt that they deserved it for the way they was treatin' people.... [The neighborhood market] is high-priced. And the money that we are giving to the stores, they're taking it to their community, Koreatown. If a black man owned the store, the money would stay among us and help us build the community up. Just because it's labeled as the ghetto doesn't mean it has to be."

At the time of the Los Angeles riots, one of every three urban blacks in the United States was officially poor; the figure for urban whites was one in seven. An inner-city household headed by a single woman stood a three-in-five chance of being trapped in poverty; and more than half of all urban black households with children were headed by a single woman. Such statistics helped explain the rage boiling over in Los Angeles and other urban areas across the nation, experts suggested. The King verdicts might have triggered the riots. "But the background is a long background of neglect," said Margaret Weir, a Harvard University social sciences professor. "It is very much a product of the neglect of the inner cities for the last 25 years."

Black Americans were better off in 1992 than they were during the Watts riots: Median incomes had risen, after accounting for inflation, and the poverty rate had fallen. But most of those gains occurred in the early years of the Great Society programs enacted during the Johnson Administration. Since 1969, the overall black poverty rate showed little improvement. And it had worsened dramatically in the nation's cities. Cut off from the mainstream economy, inner-city blacks, who once fared better than rural blacks, fell farther behind the rest of the black population. The poverty rate among urban blacks rose to 33.8% in 1990 from 21.2% in 1969, according to census figures. The poverty rate for white central-city residents was 14.3% in 1990.

In Atlanta on Friday, violence erupted for the second straight day. Students from predominantly black Atlanta University hurled rocks and bottles at police and set patrol cars afire. At least 22 people were hospitalized and 70 arrested.

Scattered protests against the King verdict took place elsewhere around the nation. Rumors of trouble sent thousands of workers home early in New York, Miami and Hartford, Conn. On 14th Street, a major Lower Manhattan thoroughfare

FRIDAY, MAY 1, EVENING HOURS
Simi Valley

I headed home to Simi Valley over strangely abandoned freeways. Pulling off the 118 onto 1st Street, I drove the rental car to the garage where my car was being worked on.

While waiting for my bill, a tanned bleached blonde in shorts and a halter top came in and announced: "They say buses of them are supposed to be coming into town tonight." "Buses of who?" the garage owner asked. "Colored people," she said. "They say they're coming up here to start a riot."

I don't know where she got her information, perhaps from the source who told my neighbor the night before that there was looting at the Target store. Coincidentally, the neighbor had just been to Target and hadn't seen a thing.

MICHAEL MOREAU
Assistant Editor,
Special Sections

117

that ordinarily caters to a bustling Friday trade, one storekeeper after another lowered iron shutters in a fearful urban domino effect until barely a window display was visible between Fifth and Sixth avenues.

Just one month before California was to vote in its June 2 primary election, the Los Angeles riots had reshaped the state's political agenda. Suddenly the issues were urban poverty, violence, law and order. The initial reaction of several experts was that the verdicts and their aftermath would help candidates who had been the most outspoken on law-and-order issues. They said any outrage and sympathy for minorities generated by the verdicts were more than offset, at least for now, by voter revulsion at television photos of looters gleefully displaying their haul.

The world, meanwhile, reacted in horror. In Libya, the state-run radio and television devoted more than half their news programs to "the *intifada* of the blacks." Japanese expressed shock at what they perceived as the deep racial divisions racking America. Both Japan and South Korea cautioned their citizens against traveling to Los Angeles, and Britain advised its citizens to be careful while visiting the city. French President Francois Mitterrand blamed conservative ideology: "George Bush is a generous man who embodies an extremely conservative political ideology, and American society is conservative and economically capitalist," he said. "Here are the results."

Two days following the verdicts, a gray-orange pall descended upon Los Angeles—a city already notorious for the nation's most polluted air. Smoke from fires limited flights at Los Angeles International Airport and brought early dusk to the city. Environmental authorities were worrying about asthma, chronic bronchitis and emphysema. The usual culprit, ground-level ozone, was not violating federal standards, but soot and smoke pushed the air pollution index near unhealthful levels in Central Los Angeles. Of particular concern were fine dust particles that carry toxics deep into the lungs—and, near the fires, the toxic substances themselves.

On Friday, as the pace of arsons slowed, a sea breeze swept in.

FRIDAY, MAY 1, 2:15 P.M.
Penn Station, New York City

Something was wrong that afternoon. I sensed it right away. This was not the same Penn Station that I ordinarily pass through to.

I wondered what was going on.

On the subway to work, I overheard snatches of conversation among the passengers: "They're beating up people on 42nd Street."

Was this all true? Was any of it?

The 4 o'clock news gave me the answer. There were no riots, no looting, no bus terminals ablaze. Nothing but a few hundred students protesting peacefully at City Hall and a few hundred others marching to Times Square for a rally.

But the news came too late for all who fled the business district in a panic-induced frenzy.

As I looked down on mid-town Manhattan from the windows of my 38th-floor office, the city was like a ghost town.

AUDREY BRITTON
Times researcher

7 BROOMS, BUCKETS, COOLING EMBERS

After three days of rage, the weekend had come and the healing began—all under the steady gaze of National Guard troops clutching M-16s.

First by the handful, then by the thousands, people of all colors, political persuasions and social status descended on the riot-ravaged streets of Los Angeles on Saturday. They came to sweep away the debris left by the days of mayhem but, more than that, they stood side-by-side with brooms and buckets in a show of hope, unity and community catharsis. Answers would come later. Now, it was time to mend a broken city.

Amid battle-scarred buildings that one minister likened to wounded soldiers, visitors like Charlie Doane, a 36-year-old movie producer from Silver Lake, came to help restore the tarnished image of the city he loved. "I'm hoping we can show the children that by helping out and chipping in," he said, "things in the future will be a little better."

Edythe Young came because she felt it her duty as a human being to help make things better. The 78-year-old Encino woman said she didn't feel comfortable staying home, by the pool, when the city had been torn apart. That just wouldn't be right.

"We want to clean up everything," explained Nam Soon Rhee, a 32-year-old Hacienda Heights resident who, accompanied by her two small children, brought a supply of brooms, gloves and trash bags. "I know we can't. But we want to try."

A jittery calm enveloped Los Angeles. Sunny skies replaced the plumes of acrid smoke. Although the embers—and tempers—had cooled only somewhat, in the minds of thousands of Angelenos, the worst was over. "This is the time for the city to be together," said 25-year-old Jonathan Kim.

It was also a time for reflection, for taking stock. For counting your blessings and your losses.

As he cleared the debris from his South Los Angeles liquor store, William Hong wondered aloud when he might reopen. Maybe by midweek, he thought. "You have to do something, you have to keep going," he said. "What else can I do? I have payments to make to the bank. I have to keep going."

As she scanned the charred remnants of her neighborhood near Vermont and Normandie avenues, 45-year-old Christina Diaz reflected on the widespread looting she had witnessed. She had no conclusions. She had seen families walking from stores holding Clorox bottles. She wondered why they would risk going to jail for that. Then Diaz tallied up what the riots had meant for her neighborhood. The Laundromat had been torched. The fish market was gone. It seemed that everything close had been decimated. Still, she was resolved to stay.

"Nobody is going to throw me out of my neighborhood," she vowed. "Yes, I've lost a part of my life here. I used to walk to Kmart, to Sav-On, to Newberry's, and I can't now. They're all gone."

SATURDAY, MAY 2, 12:45 A.M.
Western Avenue and Venice Boulevard

National Guardsmen weren't the only troops taking back the streets. A broom-wielding army of about 100 occupied the still-smoldering Venice & Western Center strip mall. Volunteers pulled rubble off the sidewalk in front of the destroyed 98 Cent Plus store.

Margit Soderlund, 54, of Pasadena worked next to actor John Reger, 40, of Marina del Rey. Morman missionaries David Adams, 20, of Pleasant Grove, Utah, and Astron Vazquez, 22, of the Dominican Republic wore soot-covered ties and white shirts. Christina Amador, 16, of Mid-Wilshire brought her mother's kitchen broom and dustpan.

Toetuu Maama, an airline cargo agent from Inglewood, brought eight members of his family. "We woke up this morning and prayed," said Maama. "People getting along together is the only way to solve this problem. That's what we prayed for."

BOB POOL
Times staff writer

A picture of Dr. Martin Luther King Jr. was placed on the burned-out skeleton of an appliance store at Hayworth and Pico by Ozell Roberson as a tribute and a reminder to the public to remain hopeful.

Photo: Marissa Roth

South Los Angeles, near the intersection of Vermont and Manchester, top right corner, was among the areas hardest hit by the violence. Every store on the east side of Vermont was gutted, beginning with a Korean-owned swap meet. In a matter of hours the blaze wiped out 42 businesses and about 120 jobs. Vermont runs from top to bottom, Manchester from left to right at the top.

Photo: Jim Mendenhall

In Koreatown, 7,000 people attended a cleanup rally on a baseball field near the intersection of Olympic Boulevard and Normandie Avenue. Prayers in Korean and English poured from the loudspeakers. "We will not retaliate. We will wait with patience. We will forgive with love."

Beginning at Slauson and Western avenues, more than 2,000 people picked their way through a five-mile-wide area, heaving chunks of rubble, fire-brigade style, into dumpsters—singing as they worked. Up the street, at Jefferson Boulevard and Western, utility crews under armed guard attempted to restore power to the traffic signals. Full power would not be restored to the city for three more days.

Carlton Shigg, a 33-year-old off-duty traffic control officer from Compton, had stopped by to help. Wearing a hospital scrub shirt and his traffic control officer's white gloves, Shigg kept the cars moving with a mime's rhythmic dancing of hands.

Many of those who came that day echoed the optimism expressed by 31-year-old Jan Marrero of the Crenshaw District: "If we can get in the muck and the mire together, then we can get together in our lives."

An estimated 30,000 people—some wearing white headbands and carrying brooms and plastic garbage bags—marched through Koreatown in a show of support for beleaguered merchants. In Seoul, meanwhile, the Speaker of the South Korean Parliament said the U.S. government should compensate Korean-Americans for riot damage.

By Saturday, the self-destructive frenzy of lawlessness had abated, ended in large part by a commanding military presence. The riot areas were patrolled by a peacekeeping force of 5,700, including National Guard, federal agents and, by that evening, 1,200 Marines from Camp Pendleton. A strict dusk-to-dawn curfew was to remain in effect throughout the weekend. Los Angeles became a ghost town after dark. Westwood Village, which normally pulsates on weekend nights with moviegoers and shoppers, now resembled an eerily lit studio back lot.

But the institutions of society were beginning to kick in. Saturday was to be the first day in court for 6,000 accused looters and arsonists, many of whom were later set free for lack of evidence or because the police could not identify them. The criminal justice system, however, was quickly overwhelmed, and by day's end only a fraction of those 6,000 cases were processed.

President Bush declared the county a disaster area, signing a declaration making homeowners, small businesses and others affected by the violence eligible for federal relief. And Mayor Bradley named Peter V. Ueberroth, chief organizer of the 1984 Los Angeles Olympic Games, to head a committee to rebuild neighborhoods ravaged by the rioting. After taking a helicopter tour of the devastation, Ueberroth vowed to make the city's reconstruction effort "a blueprint for revitalizing inner cities" across the nation.

But within hours of his appointment, some members of the very communities he would call on for help—particularly the city's ethnic communities—began questioning whether Ueberroth could effectively relate to the plight of the city's riot-torn neighborhoods. Undaunted, Ueberroth pushed forward,

SATURDAY, MAY 2, 2:30 P.M.
Post office, Vermont Avenue and 82nd Street

National Guardsmen watched the crowd, made up mostly of women and children.

One man, Jerome, claimed that when the guardsmen arrived, some were heavy-handed. He told of one—an African-American like himself—who reportedly pointed his M-16 at the crowd. "These are women and children. Why do they need to point guns?" Jerome asked, as several women nearby nodded in agreement.

Many people in line were angry. Hot day. Long wait. They said the crowd began showing up at 7 a.m. A postal worker with a bullhorn tried to keep the people calm. He asked them to have their identification ready. His remarks agitated some in the crowd and they began shouting back.

"How much longer am I gonna have to wait?" asked one.

Mike Ahern, assistant postal inspector in charge of service in the L.A. area, surveyed the crowd with a sad look. "We are trying to do the best in a bad situation. We want these people to get their checks," he said.

"It's real tragic," he said. "You have tragic stories all around here—people who are blind, people who are disabled, people who can't even get money they need for gas."

GREG KRIKORIAN
Times staff writer

At sunrise after the first night of rioting, some residents came out to see what was left of their neighborhoods. This lone pedestrian surveyed the burned-out and vandalized shell of the J.J. Newberry's at the corner of Vermont and 59th Street. Throughout the city, retail chains, including Thrifty Drug and Boy's markets, were hit by the angry crowds, though most vowed to reopen.

Photo: Gary Friedman

SUNDAY, MAY 3, 2 P.M.
Harvard Street, Los Angeles

After three nights of virtual house arrest in my Long Beach apartment, I was itching to get outside.

Thumbing through the newspaper for ideas of where to go, I noticed that the First A.M.E. Church was accepting donations of clothing and food. I had a pile of clothes—long intended for the Salvation Army—and decided to take them to where the need was immediate.

I had a little trouble finding the church. I knew I was close when I saw Range Rovers and BMWs driven by wide-eyed suburbanites looping the block. I joined the line. When I got close to the church, a volunteer peered in my window.

"Oh. You here to drop off a donation?" I told him I was. "Good," he said, and invited me to stay and help.

For the next couple of hours, I joined a disorganized but enthusiastic band of strangers loading food and clothing onto trucks bound for who-knows-where. I was pleased by the sight, but an overheard conversation broke my reverie.

"This is really nice," one church worker said to another. "But it wouldn't be necessary if just a few of these people would do this when there wasn't a disaster."

TONY MARCANO
Assistant city editor

vowing repeatedly to solicit—and heed—input from black, Asian and Latino politicians and business leaders and all others with a stake in the rebuilding effort.

By Sunday, the crisis had not passed, but the city at least made a stab at moving toward normalcy.

Many people flocked to area churches seeking spiritual strength and to hear calls for peace. In the hard-hit Korean-American community, church leaders passed out lists of vandalized businesses in need of assistance and urged forgiveness. In neighboring Ventura and Orange counties, affluent, mostly white congregants were exhorted to snuff out the racial inequalities that sparked the riots. At the First A.M.E. Church in the Mid-City area, the message was not only of regret at the damage caused by the rioting but of continuing anger at the underlying causes. "We are not proud that we set those fires," said the Rev. Cecil Murray. "But I would like to make a distinction between setting a fire and starting a fire."

As much as any place in embattled South Los Angeles, African-American churches became trauma centers for neighborhoods hard hit by the violence. From tiny storefronts to ornate cathedrals, churches were replacing the government, social service agencies and, in some cases, the family in filling the needs of people caught up in the fury. The church was where the frightened, the displaced and the desperate called first to find out how to get their electricity restored, where to get prescriptions filled or where to find a hot meal or a cot for the night. The churches organized people to help those without transportation so they could get to work or make other urgent trips. And they served as conduits for the tons of donations that poured in from around the country. They were also where distant white congregations came or phoned to offer help, and they served as town squares where politicians—including President Bush—would deliver messages of faith and hope.

On Sunday, grocery stores began to reopen. Harbor Freeway off-ramps, which had been closed through the riot zone, lost their barricades. Bus service was back on schedule. At Los Angeles International Airport, normal operations resumed as incoming passenger planes were permitted to fly over Inglewood for the first time since the violence erupted.

But despite relative calm on the streets, there were sporadic outbursts of violence. Marvin A. Rivas, who had served 10 years in the military in El Salvador, was shot to death after allegedly trying to drive his beat-up Datsun twice through National Guard barricades at Pico and Vermont. Rivas, hit by three M-16 rifle bullets, left behind a child in El Salvador and a pregnant girlfriend in the Pico-Union District.

On Monday, Bradley lifted the curfew, and the city returned to work and to school.

"It was a fun weekend, wasn't it?" Principal Randy Ward asked 150 third-graders at Whittier Elementary School in the heart of a hard-hit Long Beach neighborhood.

"No!" they hollered in unison.

Many of those displaced by the damage inflicted during the unrest were mothers and children, such as Guillermina Morena and her 2-month-old daughter, Karen. The two joined dozens of others who took shelter at Dorsey High School after their apartment on Olympic Boulevard burned down.

Photo: Lori Shepler

Some who were left homeless by the unrest escaped with their lives, but not without injury. Rafael Estrada was burned on the shoulder as he rescued his wife and dog from an apartment at the top of this gutted building. He was hurt while shielding them from the flames as they fled down the stairway.

Photo: J. Albert Diaz

"How many of you feel a little scared in your stomachs right now?" Ward continued.

Every hand in the auditorium shot up.

At Dorsey High School in South Los Angeles, students returned to find the National Guard roaming the perimeter of their campus.

With the workweek ahead, and the business of rebuilding Los Angeles at hand, a new sense of purpose dominated the collective consciousness. Yet on another level, residents from South Los Angeles to Century City reported a change—a lingering uneasiness in the way they treated each other, tensions that transcended race and socioeconomic status. The mood left blacks, whites, Latinos and Asian-Americans alike with a sense of anxiety and discomfort. This awkwardness was communicated openly and discreetly, through what was said and left unsaid, on freeways and in supermarkets, at gas stations and in lines at banks. The uneasiness was felt by everyone from the African-American who suspected that white people were locking their doors as he walked past them at an intersection to the white welder from Gardena who slept with a gun under his pillow for fear that blacks would go after him.

Amid the lingering tension, gun sales soared. The state Department of Justice would later report that in May, Los Angeles County gun dealers filed about 14,125 documents recording handgun sales, an increase of 64.3% over the 8,594 filed in May, 1991.

In South Los Angeles, fear mixed with anger—anger at what many people just called "the system."

"Rodney King is only a part of it," complained one woman who waited at a Crenshaw District bus stop, holding a shopping bag filled with empty Coke cans. "We've gone without for too long like this in this community. This was bound to happen."

Laura Price had taught her children to be optimistic. "Scripture says something good comes for those who love God," she instructed. "There's got to be something good that comes out of this for the black man."

Yet even she could not ignore the feelings of hopelessness that welled up within her when she thought about the legal system that produced the King verdicts.

"I'm not so sure that I believe a black person should believe in the system anymore, because if there are people who can sit on a jury and hear people admit to lying and then say they're not guilty for lying, how can you believe in a system? How can you believe in something you see doesn't work?"

"I don't like violence," said another South Los Angeles resident, "but I understand the frustration they [the looters and arsonists] were going through. I'm frustrated. We're all frustrated."

But that frustration-turned-rage seemed so often to be pointed at people who could least afford it. Days after flames charred one entire wing of a 54-unit apartment building west of downtown, several families were still living in the

MONDAY, MAY 4, 12:30 P.M.
Taft High School, Woodland Hills

On the first day back at school after the riots, some of the class discussions were too much for Aaron McKinney, a South Los Angeles youth who saw a large gap in understanding between black students and their white counterparts.

"We know what it's like to be persecuted because of our skin color, and they don't," said the 18-year-old McKinney, who became so upset during a discussion in his drama class that he steered himself to the back of the classroom and sat down.

Several of his white classmates had sided with the jury's not-guilty verdicts. And others, he said, even ribbed him about possibly taking part in the looting.

"They said: 'Look what you did, man,' and I'd say: 'I didn't do that!'"

"We've been stereotyped because of our skin color—they think anyone black's been looting."

HENRY CHU
Times staff writer

complex, wondering what to do and where to go. One family, afraid the bedroom ceiling would collapse from the weight of water left by firefighters, slept on soaking-wet mattresses in the living room. Their two small children coughed in air dank with mildew.

Officials estimated that about 850 families were left homeless by the unrest.

The riots also cost city residents much-needed jobs. Haydee Pinate, a 43-year-old single mother of three, lost her $5-an-hour job as a meatpacker when the market where she worked burned to the ground. "I have no savings—nothing," she said in Spanish, her arms outstretched. "All I have are my hands." Pinate was one of the estimated 20,000 people put out of work immediately after the unrest. At least 5,000 of them were deemed at "long-term risk" of not returning to work for a year or more.

And the toll was measured in other ways: the fires set, the buildings lost, the deaths. But as surviving gave way to assessing, questions were raised over just how bad things had been. Casualties eventually would climb to 60 dead and 2,383 hurt. But LAPD detectives later asserted that 15 of the deaths were not riot related. Among those were the death of a Silver Lake man who fell asleep while smoking in bed, the killing of a man who was beaten in a dispute over a few dollars worth of recyclable cans and the death of a man shot during a drug deal.

Even if the death toll were scaled back to 45, the 1992 riots still would rank as the most deadly U.S. civil disturbance in the 20th Century.

As more reliable numbers became available, officials also reduced their estimates of the number of fires and arrests. At one time, it was reported that nearly 19,000 people had been arrested. That was later cut in half. The number of arson fires, at first reported at more than 5,000, was trimmed to 623. The disparities were blamed on official reporting problems caused by the heat of the moment.

Still, at an estimated $1 billion in insured losses, the unrest was the costliest in U.S. history.

In Koreatown, the burning of family-run businesses represented not only a financial hardship but also a tragic setback and a numbing reality that maybe they hadn't come to a land of opportunity after all.

"It hurts right here," said Joyce Kim of Diamond Bar, patting her heart to describe her anguish over the reported 300-plus Korean-owned stores that were looted or set afire. "Koreatown is all our family."

"We want peace," said Myuing-Sik Ahn, 61. "We want no more fighting."

A month before the riots, Alexander Kahng had opened a Korean music store. Then the looters stormed in, causing $40,000 in losses.

"I've lived in the United States now for 29 years," said the 51-year-old merchant. "I went to college here, and graduate school, and got my doctorate here. But now, none of my experiences here seem meaningful. I wonder if, because I'm Asian, I am not really welcome in American society? I wonder whether I should leave here?"

The family of Edward A. Travens mourns the
15-year-old, who was killed on the first night
of the riots in a drive-by shooting. His father,
Allen Travens, foreground, the boy's mother,
Rosie Travens, center, and his sister, Jamie
Lee Travens, far right, attended his funeral at
the San Fernando Mission Cemetery, one
week after the King verdicts. Authorities
would later question whether his death—
and 14 others—were riot-related.

Photo: Al Seib

In a show of hope, unity and community catharsis, a multicultural army—numbering in the tens of thousands—moved into riot-torn neighborhoods after the flames were doused. Armed with grit, gumption and cleaning supplies, they descended, en masse, to hard-hit neighborhoods including this one at 85th Street and Manchester Avenue.

Photo: Joe Kennedy

As the smoke began to clear, the air filled with recriminations. The public blamed the politicians. The politicians blamed each other or police officials for responding ineffectually to the civil unrest and the conditions that spawned it.

Some said Mayor Bradley fed the riot fever with unusually blunt comments immediately after the verdicts. But by far the loudest outcry came from those who complained about the LAPD's early response or lack thereof to the violence in the streets.

By Tuesday, details began to surface about the slow response of officers at one of the early flash points of the riots—the intersection of Florence and Normandie avenues. Sheriff Block lambasted the LAPD, saying its initial response to the riots "didn't make any sense," and he accused the police of lending "an aura of legitimacy" to the looting by failing to take quick action.

City Fire Chief Donald Manning, in a report to the Fire Commission, bitterly complained that police dismissed Fire Department requests for protection during the outbreak of the riots as "not a top priority," delaying Fire Department response. "There was gridlock" on getting police protection, Manning said.

Gates fired back. Taking to the radio airwaves, he angrily blamed his department's critics for making officers so skittish about using force that they failed to move in and quell violence in the early moments of the riots. "I know police officers on the streets are scared to death to use any kind of force," Gates said, "because they think they're going to be second-guessed."

Other questions arose. Why were more than a dozen patrol captains attending a training seminar in Ventura County at the time the riots erupted? Why were hundreds of officers allowed to go home at the end of their afternoon shifts on Wednesday—even after the stunning not-guilty verdicts had been announced? Why did Gates leave police headquarters at the start of the turbulence to attend the Brentwood fund-raiser to defeat Charter Amendment F?

Gates initially downplayed his absence, saying he stayed only a short time and was in radio contact with his subordinates while on the road. But it turned out he was away for at least an hour and a half; later, he acknowledged that he should not have gone. In the first days after the unrest, Gates went from strident to subdued, but he never admitted any personal responsibility for why things went so wrong. He vehemently denied that he misjudged or failed to properly plan for the civil disturbance. "My judgment was not wrong," he said early on. "And I'm sick of answering that question. We were properly deployed."

To address the questions, the Police Commission asked former FBI and CIA Director William H. Webster to conduct an investigation. Assisting Webster would be Hubert Williams, a former Newark, N.J., police chief and president of the Washington-based Police Foundation think tank.

As for Bradley, he denied that his denunciation of the trial's outcome, broadcast live after the verdicts, played any role in provoking the riots. Bradley, however, did acknowledge that because of high tensions between himself and Gates, he had not spoken directly with the police chief in the 13 months preceding the first night of the riots. Instead, the mayor said, he communicated with the

As the embers cooled, politicians of varying political stripes came to tour the riot-torn areas. From President Bush, opposite, to the Rev. Jesse Jackson and Democratic presidential hopeful Bill Clinton, below, politicians came to get a first-hand view of the destruction caused by the worst civil unrest of the century. During his tour of a burned-out shopping center at Crenshaw and Slauson, Bush was accompanied by John Mack, president of the Urban League of Los Angeles, on Bush's right, and others.

Photo opposite: Joe Kennedy

A week, almost to the minute, after the rioting. But on this day, the scene was eerily quiet, just another burned-out intersection. Teen-ager Gemora Knox, watching traffic, talked angrily about the destruction. "We can't go to the liquor store," he complained. "We can't go around the corner to get gas."

At a beauty shop, owner Goldie Bell styled a customer's hair behind a shattered storefront window. Nearby was the charred remains of an auto shop, where Marvin McIntyre, an unemployed construction worker, stood waiting for a bus.

"A lot of us," he said grimly, "we're stuck here."

DAVID FERRELL
Times staff writer

LAPD through the Police Commission and deputy chiefs.

Meanwhile, criticism also was mounting over the slow response of the California National Guard. A top Guard general acknowledged on Monday that the first troops ordered into the riot area by Gov. Wilson were delayed for several "critical" hours by a series of decisions and breakdowns that began long before the King jury delivered its verdict. Brig. Gen. Daniel L. Brennan, the Guard's second-in-command, said his force loaned too much of its riot gear to Southland law enforcement agencies, which—anticipating problems—asked the Guard for equipment two weeks before the verdicts. He also said the lighting problems at Camp Roberts kept the force from moving its ammunition as quickly as it should have.

With a presidential primary election only weeks off, the finger-pointing even reached the national level. Critics of the Reagan and Bush administrations said a dozen years of federal neglect had spawned the crisis in Los Angeles. The White House blamed "liberal programs of the '60s and '70s." Bush later retreated from that charge and put his clout behind efforts to send Los Angeles hundreds of millions of dollars in aid.

Opponents said that just shoveling in money wouldn't solve the problem, but supporters said the money was needed to restore the face of the city. It would take much more to heal its heart.

For days, politicians of varying stripes crisscrossed the city inspecting the damage. A week after the rioting began, Bush himself disembarked from Air Force One and on Thursday, May 7, just before dawn, the presidential motorcade began a caravan tour of the riot-torn areas. Bush's inspection took him from the heart of destruction in the Crenshaw District and South Los Angeles to the burned-out furniture stores of Pico-Union and looted mini-malls of Koreatown. At each stop, he decried the violence, urging residents to look forward to the future. However, some greeted the President with skepticism and angry shouts.

"As Los Angeles comes back to its glory, all of us must ask ourselves what we can do to help," Bush said during a morning sermon at Mt. Zion Baptist Church. "…To truly help, we must understand the agony of the depressed. You can't solve the problem if you don't feel its heartbeat. You've got to understand the hopelessness of those who literally have no opportunity.

"L.A. is going to recover," he told the congregation. "It's a great city."

By Friday, the military had scaled back its presence to just 176 National Guard troops patrolling city streets. However, thousands of guardsmen remained close by, serving as back-up for battle-weary police officers. The next day, about 4,000 soldiers and Marines who had been in staging areas in Orange County left for home.

Even as the federal troops were leaving, there were sporadic outbursts of violence still being reported throughout the city. Two suspected gang members, for instance, fired at two officers in an unmarked patrol car, touching off a fusillade that left one gang member critically wounded. And, in the 77th Street Division, hard hit by the riots, officers turned up mimeographed copies of "Police Killa"

During a tour of riot-damaged Koreatown, Mayor Bradley stopped by several businesses damaged in the unrest, including a Jewelry store that was ransacked by armed intruders who shot and wounded two people. Bradley promised to do "everything we can to provide support in rebuilding," and he lamented what he called the LAPD's "lack of responsiveness" that left people "to fend for themselves."

Photo: Rick Meyer

When not relieving battle-weary Los Angeles police officers, members of the National Guard got some rest and relaxation at various staging centers in the city, including the Hollywood Bowl. The troops

flyers that were circulated throughout the area, bearing ominous threats against the Police Department.

The flyers surfaced just as some longtime rival members of the Crips and Bloods announced that they had reached a truce. "Instead of shooting each other, we decided to fight together for black power," said a 29-year-old 74 Hoover Crip called "Oz Dog." Church and community activists praised the move, while police feared possible organized retaliation against law enforcement.

On Tuesday, May 12, in a controversial show of force, special teams from the LAPD and FBI led by Chief Gates himself conducted a series of pre-dawn raids and arrested three men allegedly responsible for the beating of truck driver Reginald Denny. A fourth man turned himself in a few hours later. Police asserted that all four were members of, or affiliated with, the 8-Trey Gangster Crips, one of Los Angeles' most notorious street gangs. However, family and friends of some of the men disputed that charge.

"The Los Angeles Police Department was very, very concerned about our inability to reach Mr. Denny," Gates told a news conference. "We are hopeful that at least this will atone for some of that."

But if Gates saw the arrests as the righting of a highly publicized wrong, some segments of the community saw them as yet another affront by a system they said offered them no justice. And they waited anxiously to see if justice would come at week's end, when Judge Stanley Weisberg would decide whether to retry Laurence M. Powell, the only one of the four LAPD officers not fully exonerated in the King beating case. Powell's supporters claimed that given the climate of violence and fear generated by the riots, it was impossible for the officer to receive a fair trial.

On Friday, however, Weisberg rejected those arguments and ordered Powell to stand trial a second time. He later ruled the case would be tried in Los Angeles.

Events seemed to come full circle. What began with the videotaped beating of a black motorist led to the videotaped beating of a white motorist. A police department once criticized for brutality now was being criticized for inaction. A white police chief was about to retire, and a black police chief was chosen to replace him.

In the days following the unrest there would be much soul-searching. Televised images—of motorists being yanked from their cars and brutally beaten, of mobs looting one store after another, of fires dotting the landscape—left a lasting imprint on the public consciousness worldwide. Los Angeles had come to symbolize an ugly side of the American dream—hatred among races, a widening gap between rich and poor, the rise in urban violence and the seeming impotence of society's institutions.

THURSDAY, MAY 7, 6:15 P.M.
Blue Line station, Pico Boulevard

While their mother sat waiting for the Blue Line train, two small black boys—about 7 and 9 years old—scuffled near the train tracks.

"Cut it out," their mother ordered. The boys ignored her.

A burly, black man dressed in tattered jeans and a T-shirt approached the two boys. "Listen to your momma," he ordered. "I didn't listen to my momma, and look where it got me. I'm 42 years old and picking up bottles and cans off the street."

The boys stared at him. Immobile. "See this," he said, pointing to a tattoo on his arm. "That's my momma's name. Your momma is the only woman who will always love you, no matter what. So listen to her. Promise me. Promise me you'll listen to her."

The boys nodded their heads, yes.

"Let's shake on it," the man said. "You won't take part in no riots. You won't do no looting. You won't set no fires. And you'll listen to your momma."

The two brothers looked at each other. They each shook his hand.

The man walked away. "I'll be watching you," he warned. The two boys sat down quietly next to their mother—and listened.

BRUCE HOROVITZ
Times staff writer

Epilogue

"Let us please not go back to normal."

—Distressed caller to a radio show during the riots

After the last flames were snuffed out, Los Angeles simultaneously confronted its past and future while grappling with the present. The traumatic days of upheaval left people throughout the region—and across the nation—asking: Why did thousands of residents take to the street in rage? What conditions led to the explosion? What lessons will the city carry forward? And how will the events of April and May, 1992, shape the future?

Even as the charred, twisted remains of buildings awaited demolition, aftershocks rippled along fault lines in the social mosaic, threatening to undermine whatever fragile peace had settled uneasily over the city. Two-thirds of Los Angeles residents surveyed shortly after the riots said they believed that the city had not seen the end of the violence, that another outbreak was likely within a few years.

Pending legal actions posed perhaps the greatest threats. The Justice Department continued the civil rights investigation that could result in federal charges against the four officers in the King case. In addition, Officer Powell faced retrial on a state assault charge in the King beating, while three alleged gang members were charged with beating Reginald Denny. Some people argued that anything less than conviction for the white police officers and acquittal for the black men would be an injustice. Without justice, they warned, there would be no peace.

As the city took its first tentative steps toward healing, Chief Gates' long-awaited autobiography was released. Filled with the brashness and venom that had become his trademark, it rose quickly on best-seller lists.

Then Sgt. Stacy Koon's unpublished manuscript surfaced, laced with racial references. Philadelphia Police Commissioner Willie Williams, poised to succeed Gates, said such "disgraceful" comments would not be tolerated under his leadership.

Just days after voters approved historic police reforms prompted by the King beating, Gates threatened to stay on the job long enough to invalidate Williams' selection as chief. His action, which he later called a bluff, threw city government into turmoil once again.

On the streets, meanwhile, police kept a wary eye on the truce between the Crips and the Bloods—and clashed violently with gang members as officers broke up "unity" meetings and parties.

But none of these aftershocks had sufficient force to knock the city off the course toward recovery. Reaching out was the first step in bridging racial, ethnic and economic chasms. People gave food, clothing, money. Some traveled across the city, some across the state, to extend a hand. And many of them rediscovered that cultural diversity is more than a concept, that a population is not synonymous with a community. In some unlikely quarters, one-time antagonists haltingly sought to close the fissures keeping them apart. The truce between rival black street gangs held at least for several weeks, despite the doubts of police and other skeptics. Leaders of a Korean grocers group met with gang members, hoping to develop a rapprochement and to discuss a jobs proposal. The grocers faced withering criticism from some of their members for negotiating with "extortionists," especially while some Koreans faced bankruptcy or struggled to rebuild following the violence.

Their task, like that facing the city at large, is enormously more complex than the situation following the Watts riots of 1965. The fire this time left bigger and deeper scars. It directly touched a much larger area of the city—virtually all ethnic groups—and the impact resonated in cities across the nation. The challenge is not only to rebuild structures, but to reshape attitudes and to see whether, as Rodney King asked, "Can we all get along?" Hope itself needs to be rekindled. In the seven years since Peter Ueberroth helped organize the Los Angeles Olympics, the percentage of residents saying that things are going badly in the city rose to 85% from 25%.

Now as Ueberroth's Rebuild L.A. begins the work of helping businesses recover, several companies have demonstrated their confidence in the city by committing to rebuild quickly in areas hardest hit by the rioting, including Koreatown and Pico-Union. Sears announced that it would redesign and expand its Hollywood store, which was damaged by looters. Fedco restocked and reopened its La Cienega store in a mere 18 days, announcing, "We're here to stay." The Wherehouse record store hung a huge banner across the burned-out remains of its store on La Brea Avenue, saying, "We will be back." Other firms—Payless shoes, Taco Bell and Broadway Federal Savings among them—showed equally strong commitments to the area. And hundreds of small business applied for low-interest government loans to rebuild.

Despite the hopeful early signs, questions remained about the rebuilding effort: Would it produce significant numbers of jobs for residents of the most devastated areas? Would the rebuilding effort reflect the wishes of residents? For instance, would the rebuilt neighborhoods in South Los Angeles be saturated with liquor stores, as they were before the riots? And if liquor store owners were denied permission to rebuild, how would they be compensated?

The questions went on. With the city's schools and the state university system facing budget crises, would plans emerge for investing in the future of young people? Would there be more recreational opportunities and summer jobs for inner-city youth? Could government, particularly the Police Department, become more responsive? Accountable? Would voters regain interest in civic life and challenge their elected leaders to find new ways to confront Los Angeles' problems?

Just as rebuilding was getting under way, nearly two-thirds of the city's voters passed Charter Amendment F, the measure incorporating some of the Christopher Commission's key reforms of the LAPD.

Gates' successor, Williams, won high marks in Philadelphia as a reformer who restored trust in a department long accused of brutality and racism. Williams had publicly supported community-based policing, another key Christopher Commission reform designed to make the LAPD more accountable to the public. But in the sobering days after the riot, he cautioned, "Willie Williams is not a miracle worker. The work we have to do…is going to take time."

Time—and commitment. "Can we all get along?" That, the riots showed, would require new attitudes, new priorities. And hard work.

PERSPECTIVES

DURING AND AFTER THE LOS ANGELES RIOTS, THE TIMES PUBLISHED DOZENS OF ARTICLES CAPTURING, IN PERSONAL TERMS, THE EMOTIONS UNLEASHED BY THE EVENTS. NONE WERE MORE POIGNANT THAN ESSAYS BY ITS OWN STAFF MEMBERS THAT APPEARED IN THE NEWSPAPER IMMEDIATELY FOLLOWING THE VIOLENCE.

A woman who came of age during the Watts riot sees years of disrespect explode in anger and frustration.

BY JANET CLAYTON

In August, 1965, I was 10 years old, a then-Negro girl spending the week with her aunt, who lived near 116th and San Pedro. The Watts Rebellion—black people often deliberately call it that, not a riot—erupted nearby while I was there.

On the day after the trouble began, my aunt sent me to a store down the street to stock up on bread, meat and canned goods. "Soul Brother" signs were being nailed to stores along the way, and many of the stores were already shuttered. I didn't think much of it. I figured some people—I wasn't sure who—were just mad at each other and had gotten into a fight. I could see that everyone was nervous, though.

Soon, my parents came and picked us up. We headed home, to 75th Street near Crenshaw Boulevard, well away from the fighting and looting that was taking place to the south. We would be safe there; there would be no violence anywhere near our neat working-class neighborhood.

But there was a curfew in the riot area—and to my surprise it was being imposed on us, too. Why? Why were they treating us as if we had done something wrong?

"Janet, you are so lame," my 17-year-old sister informed me. "Why is there a curfew on us? Look in the mirror."

In fact, the curfew was imposed virtually everywhere in the city where black people lived. That's when I began to hear in my head what my Uncle Ray B used to say during Friday night political discussions in our dining room, when the adults always thought the kids were safely away, glued to the TV.

"What does the white man call a Negro with a Ph.D.?" My uncle would always pause for effect, and then draw out the answer. "A n-----. Maybe *Dr*. n-----."

Disrespect. A woman I talked to during the 1992 riots used that as a reason why she, a normally law-abiding citizen, walked into the rubble of a torched liquor store on Western Avenue and picked up a box of cigars. She said she couldn't stand the Korean-American owner. I asked her why.

"Because the first time I walked into the store he didn't say 'Hi,' or 'Good morning.' He said 'Hey, mama'—trying to talk as if he thought that's how black people talk. How dare he! He thought so little of me, thought so little of my community, that he didn't even bother to find out the most basic things about us. He took his cue, I guess, from the white people who run this country and dis' us daily. So he can take this cue: I didn't start anything at his store. But when I saw all those people in there, when I saw it was going on, I went in there and grabbed some cigars. I don't even smoke them, but somebody's gonna have a smoke on Mr. 'Hey, Mama.' "

Sound like a petty reason to gloat over a man's lost business? In isolation, it is. Except nothing is in isolation. This woman is unemployed. She is, as she described it, "pissed off a lot." There is something about not having money, and not having any legitimate prospects for getting it, that makes you mad, irritable, resentful. There's nothing race-specific about that.

But there is something race-specific about other little hurts and indignities that can pile up on African-Americans. Although many Americans really don't believe blacks still suffer prejudice, people who study these things say we do—and in consistently virulent ways. It plays out in most cities as cabbies zoom by us to pick up white passengers; as store clerks often assume we are thieves; as many whites cross the street or clutch their bags when they see a black man walking toward them.

I'm reminded of the time Condoleeza Rice, a top Soviet adviser to President Bush and a black woman, was shoved and shooed away by government agents who assumed she was a threat to visiting then-President Gorbachev. I can just hear it: "Oops! You mean *you're* with the Prez? Sorry! Here's your dignity back!"

Here in Los Angeles, the land of image-is-all and air kisses, insults are also disguised as compliments: "Gee," say astonished first-time visitors to West Adams, Baldwin Hills, View Park, Leimert Park, Inglewood or Compton, "your house is actually quite nice!" Or, the personal favorite of my husband and mine: "You two are so articulate! You speak so well!" Would any of this be surprising, or merit special comment, if two white college-educated people lived in a nice house and spoke proper English?

Under normal circumstances, thoughtless remarks are ignored. Most people don't make a big deal of it. But after the Rodney King verdicts and the resulting unrest, every slight, every rudeness, every wrong added up to be a very big deal indeed.

My niece, Angel, 23, had been watching TV coverage for hours and was fed up with it. She started shouting at the news anchor as if the two were in the same room.

"Encroach!" she said angrily. "This woman says the riots are 'encroaching on the Westside.' Give me a dictionary! Encroach means intrude. So it [the riot] belongs in our part of town, not hers. Well, forget that, lady."

What's this got to do with the riots? It's not just the verdicts in the King or Latasha Harlins cases that make African-Americans in Los Angeles, and elsewhere, feel so violated and disrespected. It's the everydayness of racism and the pretense that it is mainly a thing of the past, not of the present. Everybody loves Magic Johnson, a man few really know personally—but few want to even drive in the lane next to a car full of young black men who, in many basic ways, are much like Earvin Johnson.

Of course, a lot of African-Americans in Los Angeles don't really care whether a white person wants to drive near them, or live near them. As a matter of fact, many blacks prefer to live in areas where they can recycle black dollars to black businesses and where their children can see black authority figures— teachers, ministers, doctors, lawyers—who will set positive examples and push them to excel. That's why many blacks who can afford to live in other areas of Southern California don't move from South-Central and Southwest Los Angeles.

The "Black-Owned" signs that went up on businesses during the riots expressed more than the current version of 1965's "Soul Brother" signs. Black-owned is an assertion of 1990s "black power," with the emphasis now on economic power.

When I passed by the rubble at Vermont and Vernon shortly after the riots, I had to wonder: Why, in effect, burn down our own community and hurt ourselves just because the system—again—hurt us? Why turn the anger back on ourselves, destructively? Why commit economic suicide?

"Haven't you ever been so mad you hit your own hand and hurt it?" a friend replied. "Why is that so hard for people to understand? It's like a man who is belittled and put down by his boss constantly, and then comes home and takes it out on his wife and family. It's not right, but there's a lot of self-hate involved."

Of course the man in that example doesn't gain power by coming home and abusing his family. He gets it by finding legitimate ways to better his situation. So I felt somewhat encouraged when I saw South-Central residents—and people from other parts of the city—working together to sweep up debris three days after the unrest began.

And there was serious talk of organizing to create legitimate money-making opportunities, linking people and communities separated by the Santa Monica Freeway Divide. Dare we all hope this wasn't just another feel-good trendy thing to do in politically correct and privately paranoid L.A.?

When I was 10 and the riots hit, I never dreamed that as an adult I would relive so much of what my parents thought they were escaping when they left Texas and Louisiana. I never dreamed that schools I attended in Los Angeles in the late 1960s and early 1970s would be better integrated than the L.A. schools that will be available to my 3-year-old daughter. I never dreamed that Los Angeles would re-segregate as it has. And, I never thought that I would again see my mother scrub as she scrubbed during the 1992 riots.

I had seen her do it before; cleaning and gardening are her ways of keeping herself busy when she is upset or anxious. Gladioli sprouted in record numbers the spring after my father died; after the riots, her seeding was furious, and she couldn't seem to use enough ammonia on the kitchen floor.

Clayton is assistant editor of The Times editorial page.

A native son's affection for the city is lost amid the flames and violence. For him, everything has now changed.

BY GEORGE RAMOS

Los Angeles, you broke my heart. And I'm not sure I'll love you again.

That's not an easy thing for me to say. I know, I know—reporters are supposed to be detached observers of the routine and the unusual. Notebooks in hand, we are historians on the run, asking the obvious, repeating the answers and wondering—after the story is done—if we really understood what it was all about.

But I'm also a native son, born 44 years ago in a little hospital near the corner of 4th and Soto streets in Boyle Heights. There's an air of pride whenever I tell a listener I wasn't transferred to L.A. like some pro sports franchise.

I know, for example, that *real* baseball was played at 42nd Place and Avalon Boulevard, where the old Pacific Coast League Angels taught me about balls and strikes long before the Dodgers got here. Ask me about the people of East L.A. and I'll recite a story about somebody I met inside the First Street Store. Ask me how to get from Downey to San Fernando and I'll tell you how I was taught: Take Florence Avenue toward downtown; hang a right on Broadway and head north to San Fernando Road. Then, turn left and cruise. It'll take you a while but you'll see more of L.A. than just freeway off-ramps and billboards.

Long before Randy Newman sang it, I loved L.A.

That, I'm afraid, changed on Wednesday, April 29, when the not-guilty verdicts were returned in Simi Valley.

Everything changed.

At first, I didn't notice. I was too busy being a reporter. Right after the news broke, I interviewed dozens of folks, mostly Latinos, out on my Eastside. At the student union building at Cal State Los Angeles, a black student screamed at the TV set: "How can you look at that video and say those four white officers are innocent! Screw it! We oughta burn this city down!"

Back at the paper, I was taking dictation from reporters out in the field. They were describing frightening images—looting, arson fires, shootings—that reminded me of the violence in 1971 in East L.A. after Ruben Salazar, a Times columnist and news director of KMEX-TV, was killed during a Vietnam War protest march.

My note-taking was interrupted when demonstrators left Parker Center, the LAPD headquarters, and began trashing downtown, starting with The Times. I rushed outside, to the corner of 1st and Spring streets, to report on the destruction of my newspaper's first-floor offices, when a black man in Raiders garb pointed a gun at me.

After a tour in Vietnam, I thought I'd seen everything. In the years since my return to the U.S., I have tried to discount the increasing violence in my city, most of it the street gang variety. I guess I hoped that what I wrote about the tearful predicaments of its victims might help change things. Now, with my own life in the balance, I told the gunman matter-of-factly:

"I'm a reporter. I'm taking notes. I'm doing my job. I don't know what you're going to do but I'm going to do my job."

He didn't shoot. He just picked up a rock, flung it at The Times and ran away.

There was no time to ponder what had happened. There were more notes to take and more hot spots to check out.

By Friday morning, I was hurt and depressed. I looked at the morning edition of The Times and thought: My city is getting trashed and I can't do anything about it. The next time I say "42nd and Avalon," people will forget beloved Wrigley Field and remember instead that it's in South-Central L.A. "Hey, I'm not going there," they'll probably say.

I tossed the paper aside and started "working the phones and hitting the streets"—what all reporters do to get a *real* feel for what's happening outside the confines of the newsroom.

First, I called Middle America. I called mom.

She was moved to tears by the TV pictures of the uncontrolled beating of Reginald Denny, the truck driver pulled from his rig in the early hours of the rioting. "How could they?" she cried. "How could they?"

A native herself of Los Angeles, she went on to lament whatever she heard, saw or read about the disturbances.

"These looters never heard of Rodney King," she said. "You see these people on TV? They're proud of what they are doing. Can you imagine? Here in Los Angeles? When you start seeing a breakdown in society, laws don't mean anything. Then you start getting scared."

Mom admitted she was scared.

Then, talking like a Middle American perhaps living in Simi Valley, she reminded me that she was surprised only up to a point by the King verdicts. "I was very surprised at first, but then, after that juror talked about watching that videotape for three months, I kind of understand how they felt. They were doing their duty as best they could."

I wanted to argue, but she's my mother.

I then telephoned the home of Cristal Anguiano, the brave 12-year-old girl who risked her life to save her 2-year-old brother after she was struck in the heart by an errant bullet fired in a gang fight. I wrote about her several times in the weeks following the shooting in February, 1992. The family lives near Manchester Avenue and San Pedro Street in South-Central, and I wondered if they were OK.

They claimed to be fine, but I won't forget the tone in the father's voice. My heart sank when he said: "I want to stay in Los Angeles but we may have to go back to Mexico. The city is *loco*."

I had to agree.

Out at Lupe's modest hamburger and burrito stand on 3rd Street in East L.A., the business was brisk but the atmosphere was tense. Lupe Portillo, an aunt of one of the five La Verne Avenue soldiers I wrote about during the Persian Gulf War, said she banned any riot talk with unfamiliar customers because, "I don't know who *they* are."

"They could start something, trash the place," she said.

Wolfing down a chorizo-and-bean burrito, I wondered aloud: "Who'd want to trash this place?"

"Anybody who was *loco*," was the reply.

Things are getting bad when you can't even have a burrito and a diet soda in peace.

I drove around looking for reassurance in familiar places. Old haunts on Whittier Boulevard, Soto Street, Brooklyn Avenue and Atlantic Boulevard were safe. The First Street Store was open, though the windows were boarded up as a precaution.

Frank Villalobos cornered me after a news conference of Latino politicians at the Hollenbeck Youth Center. He is a community activist who owns an urban planning firm on Beverly Boulevard, and he wanted to remind me that there were signs of optimism in the midst of despair and depression. The landmark Sears, Roebuck & Co. store at Soto and Olympic Boulevard had been looted. But when the young culprits came home with their booty—TV sets and the like—their parents ordered them to return the merchandise to the store.

And they did so, Frank said proudly.

The ultimate dose of optimism came from Diane Gonzalez, a diminutive worker on Leticia Quezada's congressional campaign whose voice can match the roar of a jet engine. "Don't you *dare* call me a political insider," said Gonzalez, who was on leave from the staff of Democratic state Sen. Art Torres of L.A. "I'm a public servant!"

In between pushing her buttons for lively quotes, she told me not to give up hope.

"We need to return to basic values," she began. "God, government, faith in the system, family and respect. I believe in basic democracy."

She argued that those components, coupled with a new President, would make this country a more compassionate place. It would also save my town. It was hard to argue with her, especially because she was so articulate, so persistent.

But I'm not sure she was right. And it pains me to say so.

People are afraid. They talk about South-Central L.A. as if it were a territory in Libya. Before the riots, much of the city's population barely tolerated driving through those neighborhoods. Now, they will just avoid the area altogether. I know how hurtful and divisive this can be. I come from a place that has been treated the same way at times.

"Is it safe to go to East L.A. for dinner or a movie?" I am asked. "Of course it is," I thunder in righteous indignation, "East L.A. is safe. I'm from there."

Now, I'm beginning to understand why the question is asked. That is why I grieve for my L.A.

Ramos is a reporter on The Times Metro staff.

A woman who adopted this city as a student sees its myths unmasked. And she knows the rebuilding must be of the soul as well as the structures.

BY PATT MORRISON

I came here two decades ago to go to college. My mother and father ran out of fingers ticking off the reasons I shouldn't. Charles Manson. Smog. Bobby Kennedy. Bobby Seale. Earthquakes. Drugs. Watts. Freeways.

The smog was so bad that for the first month I didn't know the San Gabriels existed. Then it lifted for a brief, clear autumn moment before the Santa Anas whipped the smoke of burning shake roofs back to where the smog had been.

On the sidewalk outside the old Hall of Justice, I stepped uneasily past girls my own age, girls with shaved heads and "Xs" hacked into their foreheads, to sit in the courtroom where Charles Manson was sentenced to death, his mad eyes raking us like lasers.

I got my first bite of tear gas during the SLA vs. LAPD match. My first earthquake knocked down the shelf I had unwisely built over the head of my bed. If I hadn't already been awake, I could have been killed by my own books—just as I could have been killed by my own typewriter 10 years later, when my car got hit on the freeway. It rolled down the No. 4 lane like a big steel die, and my typewriter— which was in the back to go to the repair shop—was tossed around, too.

It missed me. But what a great reporter's obit it would have made; I repeated it with bravado.

I never told my folks that stuff. But by God, I loved it. I loved knowing where to get bialys or burritos at 3 a.m., how the SigAlert got its name, and the best songs to ask the *mariachis* to play. I loved Occidental College's Tudor rose gardens blooming absurdly below Spanish-tile roofs.

And I loved my job. In this big urban midway, journalists went everywhere, fearlessly, with the blithe air of invincibility that reporters share with teen-age boys with new driver's licenses. The only color I was, I assumed ingenuously, was the color of my press tags.

The world had L.A. pegged as the epicenter of mellow, but we knew we were tough. We inhaled particulate matter and held off brush fires with garden hoses, and clung to an Earth that tried to fling us off. We could handle anything.

All this time, it turns out, we were preparing for the wrong Big One. The Earth didn't shake L.A. apart on April 29, 1992. We did that ourselves.

Multiculturalism was the civic mantra, L.A.'s special take on the myth that I chased—we all chased—out here to the edge of the continent: There is enough to go around. My gain does not mean your loss. We can all Make It.

And every sunlit morning, mainline L.A. looked in its mirror and admired its white, educated, prosperous self, its forward-looking, tolerant self—while the other L.A. sat in the closet like Dorian Gray's portrait, getting darker and poorer and angrier.

The fissures of race and class were there, if you bothered to connect the dots. There was no citywide outcry about murdered black hookers, but when the Hillside Strangler started offing "nice" women, there was hell to pay. All of us wrote endless inner-city gang stories, but L.A. didn't "discover" gang warfare until one night in Westwood, when the cross-fire killed a young Asian-American woman. *That* raised an outcry; *that* raised a reward.

On the afternoon of Wednesday, April 29, we all gathered at the city desk to watch the verdicts read. My heart hadn't hammered in my chest like that since I took my SATs—so much was at stake here.

Not guilty? Of *anything*? *After that tape*? I must have made an odd noise, because a black friend glanced over at me. It was the look of tender pity reserved for the last kid to find out that there is no Santa. Poor Patt, it said—now you really get it.

In the days following the verdicts, scared, white L.A. got it. So this is what it's like to be incidental in a city that uses you as window dressing for its rainbow PR. This is what it's like to sit in your locked home and wonder whether the sirens you hear are on TV or right out front.

At first I was angry at the white-flight crowd who got the hell out of L.A. to escape from what one of the four cops' defense lawyers called "the likes of Rodney King," and they weren't afraid to admit it. They watched the smoke on TV from the safety of their own R-1, 3 bdr 2 ba, and said, "I told you so." They may be bigots, but at least they were honest bigots.

But then I got angrier at the other white crowd, the right-minded, PC crowd that has piously peddled a sanitized, "We Are the World" boutique multiculturalism of Caribbean music and Native American sweat lodges and Malcolm X hats on $50 blond razor cuts. They preached it at the same time they sent their kids into the safety of private schools. They signed checks at fund-raisers for justice in Central America while the Central American housekeeper at work in their kitchens couldn't afford to buy the food she was preparing.

They're thrilled to discover a new Nigerian restaurant, but they've never been downtown—let alone to Florence and Normandie. If they have, it was for the Oscars or MOCA or "Phantom of the Opera."

"Phantom" was canceled for several days after the verdicts. Another mask, a bigger one, got yanked away instead. What's underneath that one is pretty hideous, too.

I live far east of La Cienega—three blocks from Figueroa. We hear gunshots in our neighborhood, but they aren't next-door. I've bought meals for homeless women, rescued stray dogs, volunteered at my college, played pen pal to a barrio kid, picked up trash off the street.

I thought I was doing all right; to see it written down, now, it looks paltry. For the first time in a long time I felt very white and very middle class. Somebody said of Mike Dukakis that he may speak Spanish but he doesn't speak our language; suddenly, my good Spanish wasn't good enough. My glibness in English sounded mealy-mouthed and tongue-tied. I didn't feel so much fearful as inadequate.

Thursday night, Friday night, I drove around with more caution than I'd exercised in years. There was a curfew on, but the police enforcing it drove right by me. If they bothered to look twice, they just shook their heads at the foolhardiness of a white lady driving around after dark.

I hadn't cried over a story since the library burned. I didn't cry this time, until Saturday morning, when I saw the guardsmen along Wilshire Boulevard—dear, funky, passé old Wilshire Boulevard. Whatever we thought we saw in the mirror every morning, it wasn't a city fit for martial law.

We began rebuilding the week following the riots, as we would after any earthquake, but this was rebuilding soul as well as structures. I didn't hear the power brokers' standard line about multiculturalism; that record got broken on Wednesday. Instead, I saw black people rescuing a white man and Asian-Americans from a mob, and two days later, white folks in Saabs from San Fernando Valley dealerships bagging broken glass outside a gutted store on Normandie. I didn't have any idea how long it could last—maybe only as long as summer camp friendships; maybe only until the TV cameras went away.

But I did know we shouldn't get back to normal. In L.A., normal didn't work anymore. We didn't live in the city we thought we did.

On my way to work, at the corner of two empty streets, stood a scruffy young man holding a sign: "Please help—I'm homeless."

Hey, man—today, aren't we all?

Morrison is a reporter on The Times state desk.

A third-generation Chinese-American comes to a haunting realization about multiracial L.A. For the first time, she feels prejudice—and fear.

BY ELAINE WOO

On the morning of Saturday, May 2, 1992, I saw a woman wearing a T-shirt that said, "Love Knows No Color."

Fear, however, does know color. That, I'm afraid, was the rude lesson of the riots for many Asian-Americans like myself. It was a startling, deeply troubling realization.

I am a native of this city, born 37 years ago at White Memorial Hospital in East Los Angeles. I am also a third-generation Chinese-American. In my nearly four decades—living first in the Crenshaw District, then in Monterey Park and now in a community near Pasadena—I had never felt fear because of the color of my skin. Prejudice was a remote concern.

But after the not-guilty verdicts were returned April 29 against the four white officers in the Rodney King case, the city—my city—blew up in a firestorm of racial suspicions. And the whole equation of living and working in multiracial L.A. changed.

Suddenly, I was scared to be Asian.

More specifically, I was afraid of being mistaken for Korean. Having acknowledged those fears, I felt shame, guilt and an almost paralyzing puzzlement over where to go from there. Family members and Asian-American friends made these same admissions to me in the days after the verdicts—some quite gingerly because the awareness leads to all kinds of politically incorrect thought.

Ever since 1991's rash of shootings involving Korean merchants and black customers, Koreans have taken center stage in the public consciousness of who Asian-Americans are. It is not a prominence Koreans asked for or want.

But I raise it because sorting out who Asians are has become a complicated proposition over the last decade, which has brought waves of new immigrants to our city, and that sorting out is important if we are to explain the dilemma other Asian-Americans felt in the wake of the violence that rocked us to the core.

When I grew up in the 1960s and '70s, the mix wasn't terribly complex. You had your whites, your blacks, your Latinos—almost exclusively Mexican-Americans. And Asians, for the most part, were of either Japanese or Chinese descent. But as a Japanese-American colleague pointed out recently, Japanese- and Chinese-Americans no longer provide the dominant image of Asians.

Today, the Asian man from whom you buy cheap toys on downtown's 4th Street is probably from Vietnam. The pharmacist at your neighborhood drugstore could be second-generation Filipino-American. The developer who built the shopping mall where you buy frozen yogurt and submarine sandwiches could be a recent arrival from Taiwan. The attorney who handled the real estate transactions for the mall could be an "ABC"—American-born Chinese. The dentist who fixes your kid's teeth could be an American-born Korean.

Knowing the difference is important to most Asians, who want as much as anyone to be seen as individuals. But we fear our unique cultural identities still aren't recognized by non-Asians—the old "Asians-all-look-alike" trap. We know we're different from each other, but do they? Will it even matter if we're caught on a dark street with an angry person holding a weapon?

To many Asian-Americans in L.A., that is a question that haunts.

Here we are, stuck somewhere between the images of the victim and the vigilante. There was the Vietnamese man—a boat person fleeing his country only two years ago—bloodied after being pulled from his car and beaten in a South L.A. intersection. And there were the Korean shooters, brandishing shotguns and automatic weapons to protect their businesses from looters. I suspect the more troubling image for many of us was of the vigilantes.

When I raised this with my ex-brother-in-law, Rich, he blurted out straight away the awful, new truth: "I'm afraid someone is going to take me for a Korean and kill me."

Another Chinese-American friend, long involved in civil rights, expressed his anguish over the same unfounded fear.

"I feel vulnerable in the black community because of the fact they might mistake me for something else," he said. "It's that vulnerable feeling among people I respect and love that I find the most troubling. It brings out the racism in me."

A Japanese-American colleague, when she found herself thinking along similar lines, mentally kicked herself. Politically incorrect for Asians, who have tried to build coalitions. "God, that's terrible," she said. "We should try to protect solidarity with Koreans.

"But it's different now. Everybody is polarized. I find it real unsettling. What you knew, and who you thought you were, is going through an upheaval."

For a Korean-American colleague, there was hope and despair to be found in sorting through the eruptions following the verdicts.

Hyung was not embarrassed by the Korean vigilantes and did not believe other Asians should be, either. "I think we need to have that image instilled in mainstream culture," he said, "so they don't think we could be taken as wimpy Asians. What is America? It was won with guns. It was built by individuals who defended their dignity with guns. These Korean vigilantes may help balance the view of Asians. Some are gentle, some are tough enough to stand up for themselves."

A part of me winced every time the television news replayed the footage of the Korean gunslingers. But another part of me was with Hyung. I wanted to shout. "All right!" Stereotypes of Asians as wimps and nerds go up in smoke.

Of course, many Korean-Americans were appalled by the vigilantes, just as they—and so many others—could not condone the looting or other violence that impelled the merchants to take a stand. And the countervailing image of thousands of Korean-Americans marching for peace three days after the riots erupted conveyed another important and powerful message that I hope we all absorbed.

At the same time, Hyung said he could identify with the more generalized fears other Asians express. A Times photographer, he was sent to South Los Angeles on the evening of the verdicts, as the violence spiraled upward. Angry blacks chased him and hurled beer bottles and rocks at him. He fled the area when it became clear they would not let him do his job. The next day, on assignment in Koreatown, he was hassled by Latino youths, who cussed and threw gang signs at him and revved up their engines in a taunting way.

Hyung, who left Korea 15 years ago, grew up among blacks in Inglewood and lives—harmoniously, he thought—among Latinos in the neighborhoods along the Olympic corridor, was shattered by their hostility. "I think what has been happening the last few days is the ultimate expression of mistrust and distrust of each other in this city. Suddenly, I'm not welcome in the black community and I'm not welcome in the Korean community where many Latinos want to live. What is the meaning of this? Is this a sign we are supposed to get out of here? Whose land is this? Whose city is this?"

I think much of this soul-searching was peculiar to my peers in the assimilated generation, who could laugh at and feel the sting of recognition in these lines spoken by Chester in the David Hwang play "Family Devotions": "I live in Bel-Air. I drive a Mercedes. I go to a private prep school. I must be Chinese."

So when I explained to my mother how the riots served as a wake-up call that soundly disabused me of melting-pot dreams, she said of me and my four siblings, "Oh, you people never did feel prejudice."

It's true, we kids rarely encountered the open bigotry that earlier generations did. She recounted how grandpa Woo, who came to Los Angeles from China in the early 1900s, complained about laws that prevented Chinese from owning property. She recalled how, during her school days in Stockton, all the Chinese students were "stuck in a corner" of the classroom, not allowed to socialize with the whites. And how, in the late 1940s, when she and dad went house-shopping in the Crenshaw area, whites refused to sell to them.

Several years ago, when my brother decided to become a politician, mom said she warned him: "You're going to run into a lot of racism." She says he scoffed at her, told her she was being racist to even think that.

She was right, though. In campaign literature, the opposition raised the specter of "Chinatown influence" and all that it connotes. When I knocked on doors for him in Hollywood, I remember an elderly white woman shooing me away with the inevitable "Go back to China."

On a second run for the office, he won a seat on the City Council, the first Asian elected to that body in the city's history. I think he's more hopeful about the city's future than I am.

On my way from the parking garage to the office one morning shortly after the riots, I saw a young black woman striding toward me on an otherwise desolate street. In the seconds before our paths crossed, I wondered: Should I smile? Say hello? Would I do so normally? Will she be pleasant in return? Or will she say something hateful because of the color of my skin?

The moment passed, and was lost. I did not look at her. That bothered me, and will for a long time.

Woo is a Times assistant metropolitan editor.

Looking at a ravaged Koreatown, a Korean-American feels "jung"—the mingling of love, empathy and obligation that bonds his community in its pain.

BY JOHN H. LEE

My memories of Koreatown go back to the early '70s, when I was a child held captive by my mother's need for Korean sustenance. We lived in San Diego, but periodically, religiously, she took my brothers and me on a two-hour drive north to visit relatives and to shop at a little market on Olympic Boulevard near Ardmore Avenue.

At Olympic *Shikpum*, the aisles were cluttered, displays haphazard, and the American candy I liked cost more than at the supermarket.

"Why do we keep coming back here?" I asked every time, even as I enjoyed the sweet red bean of an *anko ppang* bun, a Korean-Japanese favorite. "Everything's such a gyp."

My mother always responded, "Because we are Korean."

The more practical response was that my parents wanted the food they grew up with. For years, Olympic Market was the best, if not only, place to buy Korean. My mother knew it, as did thousands of Southern California Korean-Americans.

Later, I lived in Koreatown. I was there three years ago when an accidental fire gutted the market. As customers were turned away from its charred, barred doors, there was a palpable feeling that an era had passed. News spread, and all of us who had shopped at Olympic felt a little closer in sadness, the way you do at a friend's funeral.

As I look at the Los Angeles that erupted in violence in the spring of 1992, I realize what had drawn us here went beyond the practical. I found out why my mother took pains to be part of Koreatown. Because we are Korean.

Jung is a Korean word describing the force that bonds humans to each other. It's one part love, equal parts affinity, empathy, obligation, entanglement, bondage and blood.

It is out of a sense of *jung* that we share each other's pain. The emotional drain of having seen arsonists and looters rack my Koreatown was something I suffered along with virtually every sentient Korean in Los Angeles.

If I took the feeling of loss after Olympic Market burned, multiplied it by more than 1,800—the number of Korean-owned businesses racked by rioters—then compounded that feeling with the bitterness that comes from knowing the destruction was deliberate—I would come close to describing how Korean victims felt about the L.A. uprising. Never have I felt such soul-yanking *jung* as when I reported on the victims' plight, and those who answered their pleas for help.

I collected their stories and filed them with my newspaper. Much was lost during the flurry of stories about an entire city, not just the areas that are dear to us. I saved some snapshots:

• K.H. Ahn, a former Army special forces soldier, hunched over a box of ammunition, methodically slicing a shotgun cartridge midway down the shell for the purpose of having the casing explode on impact, as I was told by Ahn. He had a Colt .45 strapped to his chest and two 20-round clips dangling from his belt.

Ahn and I spoke behind a wall of refrigerators set up behind the shattered windows and bent security bars of Cosmos Appliance Store on Vermont Avenue. A pickup truck had slammed into the locked entry way, clearing the way for hundreds of looters to descend. Refrigerators were the only merchandise left because of their size, so they became shields.

During two nights and five separate incidents, drive-by gunmen emptied hundreds of rounds into the store. The drive-bys ceased only when Ahn's group shot back.

• As the city began to sweep away reminders of the riots, funeral services were held for a son of Koreatown, killed in the cross-fire on the first night of violence. Eighteen-year-old Edward Song Lee was shot to death responding to a report of looting at a business on Hobart Avenue. Prayers for Lee expressed the grief suffered by his parents, two garment vendors living in Koreatown.

I followed the limousine that would carry the casket to the burial site. Quietly, the six young pallbearers did their duty, with thousands of onlookers clearing a swath for the procession. As the limo pulled out, and I walked alongside, I tried to remember exactly how the Korean folk saying went...."When parents die, they are buried in the earth. If your children die, you bury them in your heart." Before she entered a limousine, I glimpsed a heaving Jung Hui Lee clutching her son's photo against her chest.

As 50 cars crept onto Olympic Boulevard, I watched facial expressions in the crowd go from grim to blank. For a few moments there was stillness, then, one by one, thousands of hands began to raise and wave silently to Edward.

Jung haunts me. As do the words of Jihee Kim, niece of a Koreatown shopkeeper who lost a 15-year investment: "You have to explain how we feel."

Lee is a reporter for The Times San Diego County edition.

When fire struck, owners of some buildings did what they could to try to minimize damage —even if the effort seemed largely futile. Harry Trieu, 46, owner of Trendy Discount Furniture at 8th and Vermont streets, used a garden hose to try to keep a fire from flaring up again.

Photo: Lacy Atkins

ACKNOWLEDGEMENTS

The following provided text material and photographs that were the basis for this book:

Reporters and researchers:

Eric Bailey, Bob Baker, Sandy Banks, James Bates, Laurie Becklund, Leslie Berger, Howard Blume, Bettina Boxall, Bill Boyarsky, John M. Broder, Stephen Braun, Greg Braxton, Cheryl Brownstein-Santiago, Daniel Cariaga, Julie Cart, Mike Castelvecchi, Irene Chang, Stephanie Chavez, Mathis Chazanov, Frank Clifford, David Colker, Rich Connell, Michael Connelly, Miles Corwin, Richard Cromelin, Tina Daunt, Paul Dean, Maura Dolan, David Dorion, Sylvie Drake, Tammerlin Drummond, Norman Duarte, Ashley Dunn, Petula Dvorak, William J. Eaton, Ken Ellingwood, Virginia Ellis, Paul Feldman, David Ferrell, Andrea Ford, David J. Fox, Ralph Frammolino, David Freed, Mary Lou Fulton, Sam Fulwood III, Tom Furlong, Laura Galloway, Kenneth J. Garcia, James Gerstenzang, Jerry Gillam, Mark Gladstone, Larry Gordon, Gary Gorman, Jill Gottesman, Nina Green, Tina Griego, Martha Groves, Wallace Guenther, Lee Harris, Ron Harris, Scott Harris, Steve Harvey, George Hatch, Melissa Healy, Nieson Himmel, Bernice Hirabayashi, Bruce Horovitz, Shawn Hubler, John Hurst, Carl Ingram, Sam Jameson, Douglas Jehl, Sherry Joe, Ted Johnson, Charisse Jones, Robert A. Jones, Jesse Katz, Amy Louise Kazmin, Daryl Kelley, Roxana Kopetman, Kim Kowsky, Greg Krikorian, Marc Lacey, David Lauter, Don Lee, John H. Lee, Patrick Lee, Dave Lesher, Eric Lichtblau, Paul Lieberman, John Lippman, Carlos V. Lozano and Maureen Lyons, Hugo Martin, Penelope McMillan, Patrick J. McDonnell, Jean Merl, Victor Merina, Josh Meyer, Michael Meyers, Judith Michaelson, John L. Mitchell, Suzanne Muchnic, Frederick M. Muir, Thomas S. Mulligan, Dean E. Murphy, Edmund Newton, Jim Newton, Myrna Oliver, Lisa Omphroy, Ronald J. Ostrow, John O'Dell, Santiago O'Donnell, Richard O'Reilly, Michael Parrish, Psyche Pascual, Judy Pasternak, James F. Peltz, Jonathan Peterson, Tom Petruno, Chuck Phillips, Art Pine, Bill Plaschke, Mark Platte, Bob Pool, Terry Pristin, Claudia Puig, Amy Pyle, Michael Quintanilla, Janet Rae-Dupree, Jeffrey Rabin, James Rainey, Cecilia Rasmussen, Mack Reed, Kenneth Reich, James Risen, Andy Rivera, Carla Rivera, Anne C. Roark, Ted Rohrlich, Ron Russell, Louis Sahagun, D'Jamila Salem, Robert Scheer, Deborah Schoch, John Schwada, Richard A. Serrano, Jube Shiver Jr., Douglas P. Shuit, Bob Sipchen, Claire Spiegel, Stuart Silverstein, Richard Simon, George Skelton, Phil Sneiderman, Shauna Snow, Bill Stall, Larry B. Stammer, Edith Stanley, Sheryl Stolberg, Dean Takahashi, Julie Tamaki, Tracy Thomas, Hector Tobar, Vicki Torres, David Treadwell, William Tuohy, Mike Utley, Cynthia Viers, Amy Wallace, Mike Ward, Jenifer Warren, Jonathan Weber, Dan Weikel, Henry Weinstein, Daniel M. Weintraub, George White, Irene Wielawski, Tracy Wilkinson, David Willman, Tracy Wood, Chris Woodyard, Eric Young and Nora Zamichow

Photographers and lab technicians:

Lacy Atkins, Aurelio Jose Barrera, Larry Bessel, Todd Bigelow, David Bohrer, Gerard Burkhart, Bruce Cox, Harold G. Crawford,Jr., Larry Davis, J. Albert Diaz, Patrick Downs, Alan Duignan, Steve Dykes, Gary Friedman, Guy Goodenow, Robert Gabriel, Lawrence K. Ho, Hyungwon Kang, Rosemary Kaul, Joe Kennedy, Kathy Kottwitz, Ken Lubas, John Malmin, Kirk McKoy, Mike Meadows, Jim Mendenhall, Matt Randall, Rick Meyer, R.L. Oliver, Marissa Roth, James Ruebsamen, Iris Schneider, Al Seib, Lori Shepler, Marilyn Weiss and Mike Zacchino

Technical support:

Jim Angius and John Drom